PORTRAIT OF A TRAGEDY

JAMES A. WARREN

PORTRAIT OF
AMERICA AND THE

A TRAGEDY
VIETNAM WAR

LOTHROP, LEE & SHEPARD BOOKS

NEW YORK

For my parents, David and Grace Warren

Maps drawn by Teresa Bonner

Copyright © 1990 by James A. Warren
Printed in the United States of America. First Edition 1 2 3 4 5 6 7 8 9 10

Library of Congress Cataloging in Publication Data
Warren, James A. Portrait of a tragedy : America and the Vietnam War / James A. Warren.
    p.   cm.   Bibliography: p. Summary: A discussion of the causes, events, and aftermath of the longest and most controversial conflict in American history.   ISBN 0-688-07454-5.
1. Vietnamese Conflict, 1961–1975—United States—Juvenile literature. [1. Vietnamese Conflict, 1961–1975.]   I. Title. DS558.W38   1989 959.704'33'73—dc19
88-39560 CIP AC

ACKNOWLEDGMENTS

A number of people provided assistance of one sort or another in the writing of this book. Richard Davis was the first person with whom I discussed the idea of a history of the Vietnam War for teenagers, and it was Richard who put me in contact with Dorothy Briley, my editor, who believed in the project from the very beginning. I am grateful to them both.

My discussions over the past five years with Colonel Harry G. Summers, Jr., have helped to clarify many of the complexities and ambiguities of the war. Shelby L. Stanton provided a number of rare photos and was generous with his time. Historian John A. Scott offered encouragement throughout in addition to providing me with a number of excellent books written by the Vietnamese on the war. Michael O'Shea, ex-marine infantryman, shared his experiences of fighting against the North Vietnamese near the DMZ on a number of occasions. I am particularly grateful to William D. Neal, former U.S. Army officer and veteran of two tours in Vietnam. Bill shared both his personal combat experiences and his ideas on the war's controversial issues most generously. He read the manuscript and provided me with invaluable comments and suggestions. My brother, Paul Warren, helped me refine some of the ideas expressed in this history. Special thanks to Britta Goossen, who has for years cheerfully endured my obsession with Vietnam. Without Britta's encouragement and support the book would never have been finished.

ASIA DURING THE VIETNAM WAR

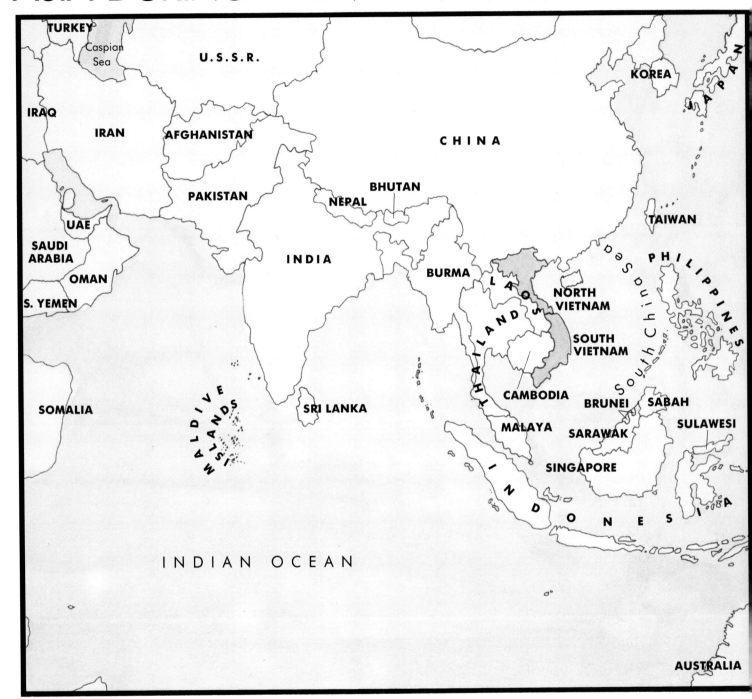

Contents

FOREWORD

Even for those who served there, the Vietnam War is hard to understand fully. One reason is that it went on for so long. Compared to the less than four years the United States was involved in World War II, or the three years we were involved in the Korean War, our Vietnam involvement lasted almost twenty-five years.

That almost guaranteed distortion, for the attitudes, expectations, and certainties common in September 1950, when the first U.S. military advisory team was sent to Vietnam, were not those most Americans shared a quarter-century later when the last U.S. helicopter lifted off the roof of the American Embassy in Saigon on April 30, 1975.

And even for the more than two and one-half million American men and women who served within the borders of South Vietnam during those twenty-five years, the war was very much time and space dependent. For example, a soldier who served as an adviser to South Vietnamese military forces in the southern tip of South Vietnam in the Mekong Delta in 1959 fought an entirely different war than the soldier or marine who served in the mountainous northern portion of South Vietnam along the Demilitarized Zone in 1969.

One fought a war against black pajama–clad Vietcong guerrillas armed with primitive weapons. The other fought a war against uniformed North Vietnamese Army regulars armed with sophisticated weapons, backed up by tanks and artillery. The war in the Delta was a counterinsurgency war, the war along the DMZ was virtually a reenactment of the trench warfare of the First World War. But, different as they may have been, both represented the "truth" about Vietnam.

Another factor that made the war hard to understand at the time was the intensity of the emotions the war evoked. Those opposed to the war as well as those who supported it tended to emphasize those facts that reinforced their point of view and slight those that did not. Thus much of what was written and said then tends to be so ideologically skewed that it obscures more than it reveals.

Time, however, has cooled those passions and allowed a more balanced picture to emerge. Aptly named, *Portrait of a Tragedy: America and the Vietnam War* accurately portrays the war's complexity and diversity in clearly written, even-handed and straightforward terms free of ideological cant and distortion. With a refreshing departure from most Vietnam War literature, James Warren respects his readers by presenting the facts and allowing them to reach their own conclusions. Thousands of books have been written on the Vietnam War, but here is the best place to start.

Harry G. Summers, Jr.
Colonel of Infantry, U.S. Army (Ret.)

PREFACE

The Vietnam War, or the Second Indochina War, as it is some-times called, was the longest and most controversial conflict in American history. Because the government of the United States never officially called the conflict in Vietnam a war, it's hard to say just when it began. The first official American deaths in Vietnam oc-curred in 1959. Although very few Americans died in the jungles of Southeast Asia until 1965, when the first combat units were sent there, the U.S. government supplied the French with money and equipment to fight the Vietnamese communists in their war, which began in 1946, and continued to support anticommunists in Viet-nam up to 1975.

All wars are complex, brutal affairs that test the endurance of soldier and ordinary citizen alike. The Vietnam War, in which the United States, its allies, and South Vietnam fought against rebels within South Vietnam called the Vietcong and communists from North Vietnam, tested the endurance and the understanding of the American people in ways that other wars have not.

As an episode of military history, Vietnam is really just begin-ning to be explored, and its importance goes far beyond military history. The American experience in Vietnam provides us with a wealth of clues and insights about modern American history and American values. When President John F. Kennedy was laying the groundwork for direct American intervention in Vietnam in the early 1960s, the United States had reached the height of its power and self-confidence. We were the unchallenged leaders of the free world. There was a belief among the nation's leaders that the United States was invincible, that it had not only the political and military might to do what it wanted where it wanted, but also the moral authority to do so.

In 1975, Americans watched on television the humiliating evacuation of Saigon, the capital city of South Vietnam. The surrender of the city to the communists ended a terrible era in our history— an era that had changed us. America was an entirely different nation than it had been back in the early 1960s. We were no longer so sure of our path, no longer confident that we had the answers to all the important questions.

The war had come close to tearing the nation apart. The American public no longer trusted its government. The armed forces of the nation had become demoralized and fragmented. The soul and conscience of the nation had been deeply wounded. And more than 57,000 men had sacrificed their lives in what is now thought to be a dubious crusade.

How did it all happen? Why? Read on, and find out about a great American tragedy—the war in Vietnam.

ABBREVIATIONS AND SPECIAL TERMS

ARVN Army of the Republic of Vietnam. The regular army of South Vietnam.

battalion A military unit numbering from 500 to 900 men, depending upon the unit's function.

brigade A military unit of approximately 3,000 men.

CINCPAC Commander in Chief, Pacific Command. Commander of American military forces for the Pacific, including the entire Indochina region.

company A military unit of approximately 140 soldiers.

COMUSCAV Commander, United States Military Command, Vietnam.

division A military unit of approximately 20,000 men.

DMZ The Demilitarized Zone. A designated area between South and North Vietnam that was supposed to be closed to the military forces of either. It was an area of heavy fighting.

DRV Democratic Republic of Vietnam; North Vietnam.

free-fire zone Territory where unlimited use of firepower was permitted by the government of South Vietnam.

GVN Government of Vietnam (South Vietnam).

JCS The Joint Chiefs of Staff, a body composed of the chiefs of staff of the United States armed services—Army, Navy, Air Force, and Marine Corps.

LZ Landing zone. A designated area where helicopters could land and unload troops.

MAAG Military Assistance Advisory Group. The U.S. organization set up in 1950 to assist the French in Vietnam.

MACV Military Assistance Command, Vietnam. The top U.S. military command in Vietnam from 1962 on.

military tactical zones The U.S. military divided South Vietnam into four military regions known as tactical zones. Running north to south, they were designated I Corps, II Corps, III Corps, and IV Corps.

NLF National Liberation Front. The political organization of the communists in South Vietnam, created in Hanoi in 1960 by the North Vietnamese Communist Party.

NVA North Vietnamese Army.

platoon A military unit of approximately forty men.

PRG Provisional Revolutionary Government (of the Republic of South Vietnam). Formed by the NLF and other anti-GVN factions as an opposition government.

third world The group of nations, many of them underdeveloped, that are not firmly aligned with either the Eastern or the Western political bloc.

VC Vietcong, the communist insurgents who fought against the GVN and the Americans. They were the military arm of the NLF.

PORTRAIT OF A TRAGEDY

SOUTH VIETNAM:
Provinces, Major Cities, Battles, and Regions

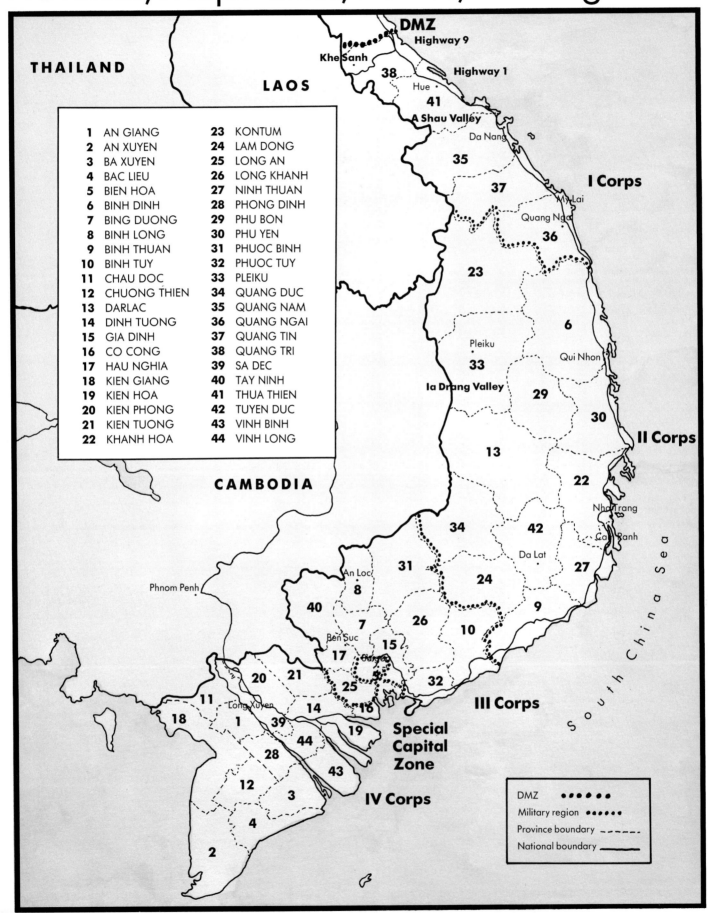

1 AN GIANG	23 KONTUM
2 AN XUYEN	24 LAM DONG
3 BA XUYEN	25 LONG AN
4 BAC LIEU	26 LONG KHANH
5 BIEN HOA	27 NINH THUAN
6 BINH DINH	28 PHONG DINH
7 BING DUONG	29 PHU BON
8 BINH LONG	30 PHU YEN
9 BINH THUAN	31 PHUOC BINH
10 BINH TUY	32 PHUOC TUY
11 CHAU DOC	33 PLEIKU
12 CHUONG THIEN	34 QUANG DUC
13 DARLAC	35 QUANG NAM
14 DINH TUONG	36 QUANG NGAI
15 GIA DINH	37 QUANG TIN
16 CO CONG	38 QUANG TRI
17 HAU NGHIA	39 SA DEC
18 KIEN GIANG	40 TAY NINH
19 KIEN HOA	41 THUA THIEN
20 KIEN PHONG	42 TUYEN DUC
21 KIEN TUONG	43 VINH BINH
22 KHANH HOA	44 VINH LONG

THAILAND

LAOS

DMZ
Highway 9
Khe Sanh
38
Highway 1
Hue
41
A Shau Valley
Da Nang
35
37
I Corps
My Lai
Quang Ngai
23
36
6
Pleiku
Qui Nhon
33
29
Ia Drang Valley
30
13
II Corps
22
Nha Trang
Cam Ranh
CAMBODIA

34
42
Da Lat
31
An Loc
24
27
8
Phnom Penh
40
9
7
26
10
Ben Suc
15
17
Saigon
32
20
21
25
III Corps
11
Long Xuyen
14
16
18
1
39
19
Special
Capital
Zone
44
28
12
43
3
IV Corps
4
2

South China Sea

DMZ	••••••
Military region	••••••
Province boundary	– – – –
National boundary	————

1. A Place Called Vietnam

When World War II ended, Vietnam meant almost nothing to the people of the United States. Had most Americans been asked to find this ancient Asian country on a map, they probably wouldn't have known where to begin. Americans knew so little about Vietnam in part because it was on the other side of the earth from the United States—about 9,000 miles from Washington, D.C. But distance wasn't the only reason for our ignorance. In the 1940s, the word "Vietnam" couldn't be found on a globe or in an atlas, at least not one in English. Vietnam, located along the coast of the Indochinese peninsula south of China, had been stripped of its name by its Western colonizers, the French. Masters of Vietnam since the 1880s, the French had lumped the country in with its neighbors, Laos and Cambodia, under the name French Indochina.

In 1945, when the great powers of the world were deciding the fate of the areas that had been taken over by Germany and Japan before the Allied victory, there was some doubt about what to do with the former European colonies. France, occupied and humiliated in the recent world war and anxious to regain her prestige, was determined to retain her influence in Southeast Asia, despite all the talk about the right of all peoples to forge their own destiny, independent of outside interference.

To the American foreign policy experts, and indeed to President Harry S Truman, Vietnam was an obscure parcel of land, a French colony whose people were culturally akin to the Chinese. The Americans knew little of the realities of life in Vietnam. However,

17

Rice farming has shaped the lives of all Vietnamese for centuries. Here, two farmers irrigate a rice paddy by hand before planting season. (U.S. Marine Corps photo.)

they were very much aware that France would soon once again be an important player in world politics and that French cooperation would be needed in the struggle between the communist and democratic worlds. So the United States supported the French in their return to power in Indochina.

The decision was hardly an issue of major concern for most Americans. Its consequences, of course, were not known to those who made it. But those consequences would be staggering, for the decision to support French claims in Indochina began America's long and tragic involvement in Vietnam. Had the Americans known more about the history of French colonialism in Vietnam, the Vietnam War might never have happened.

French involvement in Southeast Asia began in the seventeenth century, when missionaries journeyed there to spread the word of the Catholic Church. The priests came back with tales of vast riches, and soon adventurers and traders were lured to Vietnam's shores.

The Confucian mandarins, or public officials appointed by the emperor, who governed Vietnam were wary of the intruders, believing that the Westerners were little more than barbarians. But they were also fearful of France's military power, and so they reluctantly granted trading rights. By the middle of the eighteenth century, the French, disturbed by the growing British influence in Asia, were determined to take over all of Indochina (Vietnam, Laos, and Cambodia).

The continued repression of Catholic missionaries by the Vietnamese officials gave France the pretext that it needed to invade Vietnam, which it did in 1858. Over the next thirty years, the invaders stripped the Vietnamese emperor and his mandarins of all real governing power. By 1890, through the use of brutal force and political maneuvering, France established control not only over Vietnam, but over Laos and Cambodia as well.

The French presence brought upheaval in Vietnamese society. For well over a century the Vietnamese had resisted contact with the West, despite the increasingly aggressive French policies. Now a Western nation ruled their ancient kingdom with an iron hand. For centuries, Vietnam had been governed by the Confucian-trained mandarins, men of great learning who studied the ancient Chinese texts for answers to all social and ethical questions. The Confucian political philosophy was cast aside by a new ruling class, composed of French military men and administrators. A harsh code of justice—completely unintelligible to the Vietnamese—was installed.

The peasantry were stripped of their precious plots of land, putting the cultivation of rice (Vietnam's major crop) in the hands of landlords sympathetic to the French. The dispossessed were put to work in industries producing rubber, tin, and coal to make France's colony profitable. The conditions under which these workers toiled were ghastly. Men, women, and children alike labored until they dropped from overwork, malaria, or malnutrition.

How was it possible for a supposedly civilized nation to rule so cruelly? For one thing, the French, like the other great Western pow-

Expansion of the French Indochina Union

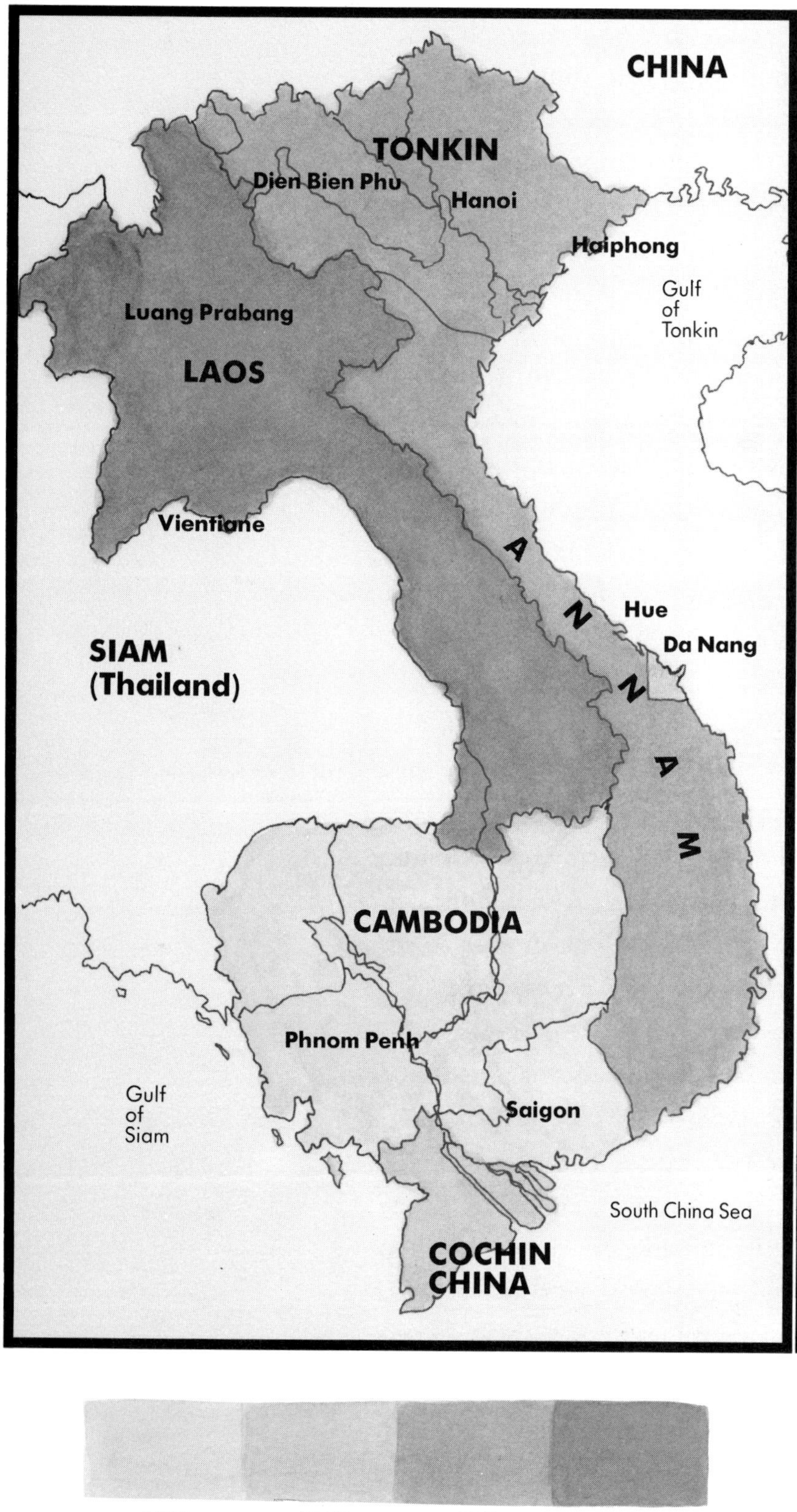
CHINA
TONKIN
Dien Bien Phu
Hanoi
Haiphong
Gulf of Tonkin
Luang Prabang
LAOS
Vientiane
ANNAM
Hue
Da Nang
SIAM (Thailand)
CAMBODIA
Phnom Penh
Saigon
Gulf of Siam
South China Sea
COCHIN CHINA
1863
1867
1883
1893

Geographical Features of Vietnam

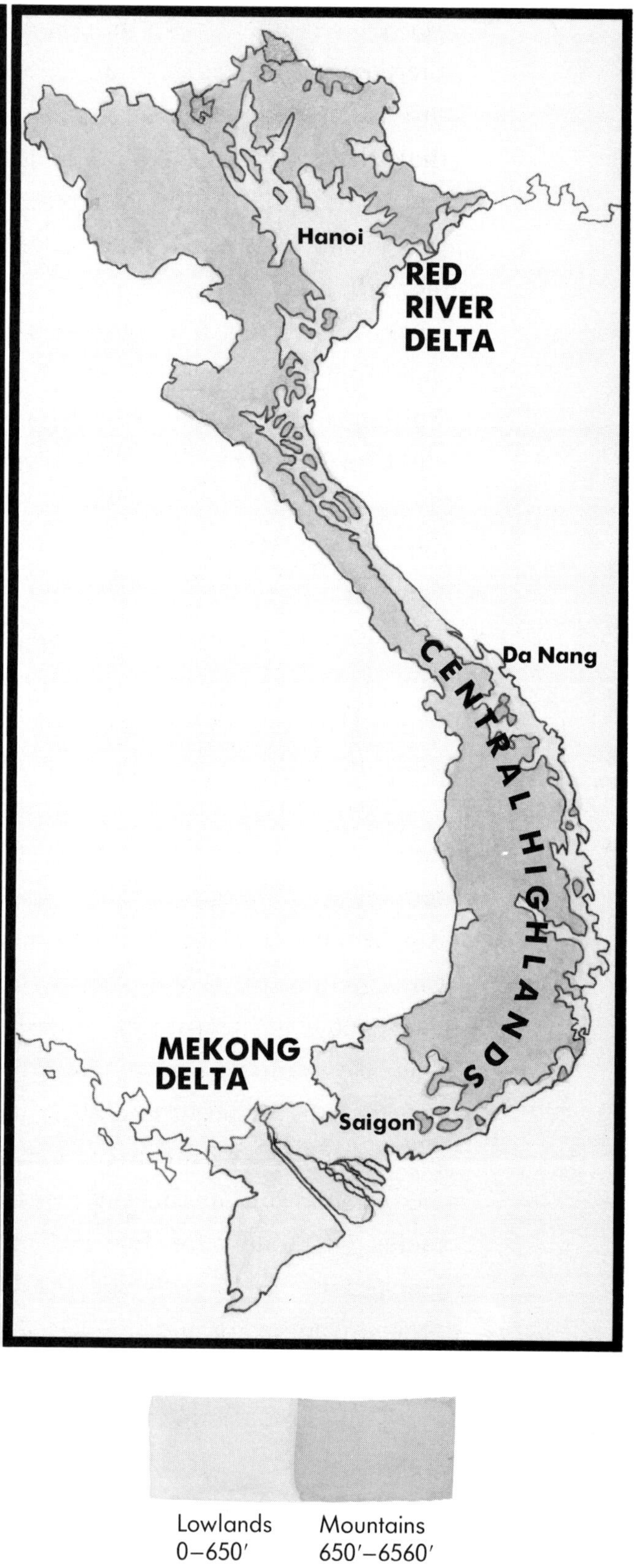
Hanoi
RED RIVER DELTA
Da Nang
CENTRAL HIGHLANDS
MEKONG DELTA
Saigon
Lowlands 0–650′
Mountains 650′–6560′

ers, felt their way of life to be vastly superior to the cultures of Asia. Many Frenchmen in Vietnam honestly believed they were doing the Vietnamese a great service. Were not the laws, literature, architecture, and government of France the best in the world, far better than those of the east? There was even a phrase for the French objective: *mission civilisatrice*, or "civilizing mission."

In short, the French, believing that the Vietnamese were little more than savages, sought to banish all the nation's institutions and customs, despite the fact that Vietnam had a more ancient heritage than France did. It was in many ways a policy like that which white Americans inflicted on the North American Indians. It sought to eliminate an entire way of life. It was the worst form of imperialism.

Given the utter disregard for the welfare of the people of Vietnam shown by the French, it was hardly surprising that resistance and protest spread. In the early years, Vietnamese rebels had ambushed French troops in the mountains. But France's real enemy in its effort to exploit Vietnam wasn't rebel troops. Rather, it was a growing sense of nationalism among the Vietnamese elite which took shape in the 1920s and 1930s.

Nationalism, briefly defined, is the idea that the people of a nation have a right to shape their own destiny without outside interference. Throughout the course of the 1920s and 1930s, nationalism became a potent force and rallying cry for colonized peoples throughout Asia. It was particularly strong in Vietnam, as the Vietnamese had a long history of independence, and because French rule was so venal and destructive. With every act of French brutality, the Vietnamese will to resist got stronger.

A number of different schools of Vietnamese nationalism gathered momentum as the 1930s wore on. Some pointed to the democracies as models for future Vietnamese independence. Was not France's control over its colony an outrage when a great war—World War I—had been fought, in the words of President Woodrow Wilson of the United States, to make the world "safe for democracy"?

The democratically inclined nationalists, however, were neither as sophisticated nor as well organized as the burgeoning Indo-chinese Communist Party. The leader of the communists in Indochina, a native of Vietnam who had left the country in 1911 to gain his education and lobby for the independence of the Indochinese colonies, was Nguyen That Thanh. Over the years he adopted several aliases. Eventually he would become known the world over as Ho Chi Minh, which means "he who enlightens." He was the father of Vietnamese communism and the most prominent nationalist in the fight against the French.

Ho's party had been formed in 1930 in Hong Kong, and had agitated and organized for independence throughout the decade, establishing student groups and spreading the doctrine of communist

An early photograph of the father of the Indochinese Communist Party, Ho Chi Minh. (Camera Press Ltd. photo.)

revolution wherever possible. In 1941, after the Japanese had marched into Vietnam and taken control from the French (who had been defeated by Nazi Germany by then), Ho slipped quietly back into the country for the first time in thirty years. He met with other key Vietnamese communists, notably Pham Van Dong and Vo Nguyen Giap, and established the political and military organization designed to bring communist revolution to his native land. It was called the Viet Nam Doc Lap Dong-Minh (League for the Independence of Vietnam), and its adherents were known as the Vietminh.

Some students of Vietnamese history have claimed that the Vietminh were not firmly committed to communist rule in the early years of the struggle. The truth is that many of the Vietminh were not communists. But the leaders of the organization were all "professional revolutionaries," as Ho once referred to himself. Their ultimate goal was not just Vietnamese independence. It was a Vietnam governed by the Communist Party.

In the chaos that followed the Japanese surrender, the Vietminh outclassed the rival nationalist groups in Vietnam and proved shrewd enough to seize power immediately after the Japanese were vanquished. As we shall see, the French had no intention of allowing Ho to remain in control of Vietnam without a fight. Vietnam was about to become a battleground.

Ho Chi Minh, leader of the Vietminh and father of the Indochinese Communist Party, was not a very imposing figure, face to face. Small and fragile, he looked more like a shy schoolteacher than a professional revolutionary.

Ho was born in central Vietnam in 1890, the son of a mandarin of the emperor's court. From his earliest adult years, Ho was committed to the cause of freeing Vietnam from the shackles of French colonialism. In 1919, he made a plea for Vietnamese independence to the great powers at the Versailles Conference, which ended World War I. Those who heard him deliver his speech for independence were impressed by his determination and great conviction. In the

THE HO CHI MINH TRAIL

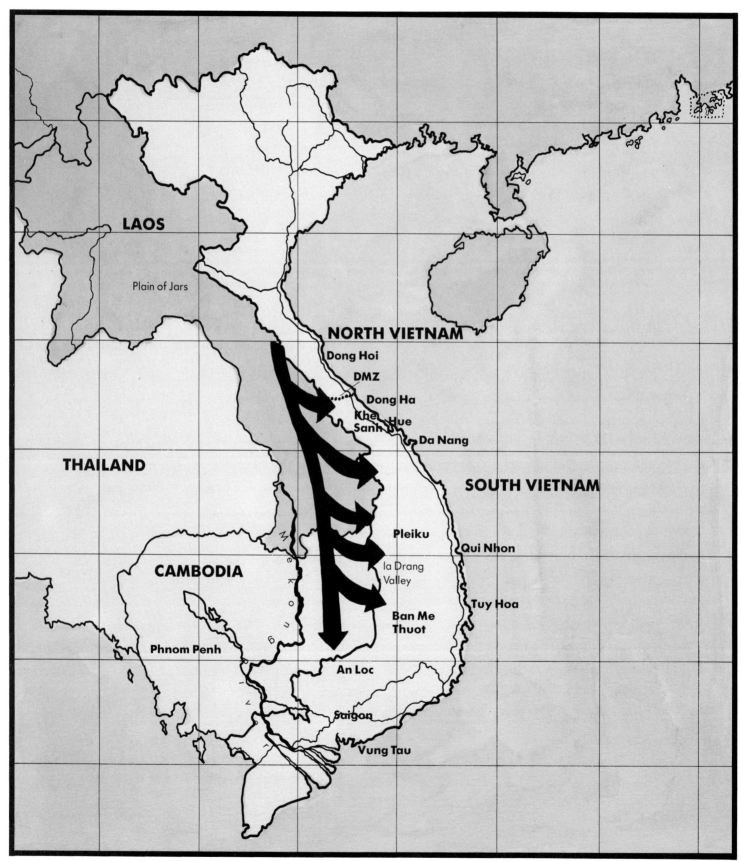

LAOS

Plain of Jars

NORTH VIETNAM

Dong Hoi

DMZ

Dong Ha

Khe Sanh   Hue

Da Nang

THAILAND

SOUTH VIETNAM

Pleiku

Qui Nhon

Ia Drang Valley

CAMBODIA

Tuy Hoa

Ban Me Thuot

Phnom Penh

An Loc

Saigon

Vung Tau

Mekong

few photographs of Ho which remain from this time in his life, his passion shows not so much in the way he held himself—for even then he was a frail-looking man—but in his eyes.

By the time Ho stood in front of a huge crowd in Hanoi on the morning of September 2, 1945, to declare Vietnam a free and independent state, he had spent thirty-five years traveling, fighting, and learning. In Paris he had learned about modern Western political ideas and culture. He had received political training in Moscow, and had spent a good deal of time in China as well, working with Mao Zedong, the leader of Chinese communism.

Now it appeared as though the long years of struggle had paid off. For on the morning of September 2, there was much rejoicing. The war against Japan was over, and the political vacuum which had been created by Japan's defeat had given the Vietminh a fighting chance to gain power in their country and to keep it. But their hopes were soon dashed by the victorious Allies, who had little liking for any government supported and led by communists. The British, who were responsible for administering Vietnam south of the 17th Parallel immediately after the war, promptly declared martial law, rearmed the French garrison (which had been under the control of the Japanese), and forced the Vietminh out of Saigon's city hall, where they had established their government. In the north, particularly near the city of Hanoi, Ho's power was greater, but he still had to wrangle with the Chinese, who were supposed to be restoring order north of the 17th Parallel.

The actions of the Allies disheartened Ho and his followers, but they continued in their effort to establish themselves as the true government of Vietnam.

Unfortunately for the Vietminh, the French admiral placed in charge of France's affairs in Vietnam, Thierry d'Argenlieu, had little interest in granting the Vietminh anything, let alone the control of a French colony. D'Argenlieu spoke for many Frenchmen when he wrote to the general commanding the French expeditionary force in Indochina: "I am amazed—that is the word, amazed—that France's fine expeditionary corps in Indochina is commanded by officers who would rather negotiate than fight."[1]

The French saw Vietnam's independence as existing only *within* the French union of nations. This meant that while the Vietnamese would be able to run their own domestic political affairs, the French would be responsible for controlling defense and all foreign policy. To the Vietminh, and to other Vietnamese nationalists as well, this was no independence at all.

This fundamental disagreement on the meaning of independence became more apparent as negotiations proceeded at conferences in Dalat (a small city in central Vietnam) and Fontainebleau (a town near Paris) in the spring of 1946. Whatever chance there had been for compromise—and therefore peace in Vietnam—faded quickly.

On November 20, French and Vietnamese troops clashed in the port of Haiphong. At first there were only small firefights, but then the French navy went into action, shelling the city into submission and killing thousands. On December 18, the Vietminh responded, launching attacks against French military posts around the entire country. The First Indochina War had begun.

The French, exuding confidence and showing astounding ignorance of the situation in Vietnam itself, predicted a short war. The insurgency, the generals said, would be crushed by superior firepower, and Vietnamese independence would be established according to French dictates. But the war took eight long years, and when it was over, France had suffered a humiliating defeat, Vietnam was divided at the 17th Parallel by a treaty, and the groundwork was laid for America's war in Vietnam.

The First Indochina War was not a conflict with large battles, such as those in the world war which had just preceded it. It was in many ways a more difficult war for the soldiers who fought there than World War II had been, because in Vietnam, there was no single front, no one place where armies met and did battle. Like so many of the wars which had shaped Vietnamese history since there

Jean de Lattre de Tassigny, the French commander in Indochina in 1950–51. He improved French morale greatly, leading to the defeat of the Vietminh in several key battles. (E.C.P. Armées.)

had been a Vietnam, the war between the French and the Vietminh was largely a guerrilla war.

The Vietminh were determined and skillful fighters, and they believed strongly in their cause. During the first years of the war they inflicted some humiliating defeats on the heavily armed French troops, who were unable to control the rural areas of the country. In late 1950 and 1951, French troops rallied behind a great general, Jean de Lattre de Tassigny, and for a while at least, the war seemed to be going France's way.

By the time of the general's arrival, however, the First Indochina War had taken on an entirely new dimension, making its outcome something of great concern not just to France, but to all of the Western alliance. China had become a communist nation, giving the Vietminh a great boost, as they could now depend upon a steady flow of supplies from their neighbor to the north. The Korean War had broken out, with United Nations–sponsored soldiers fighting communist North Koreans. Communist insurgencies in other

Asian countries such as Malaya, Burma, and Indonesia led to increasing resolve to halt the advance of communism.

The French, already drained by four years of war, needed help, and they saw that the tense situation that existed at the time between the forces of democracy and communism would ensure that such help would be forthcoming from the country most concerned about the spread of communism: the United States.

From the end of World War II, America had been thrust into the role of leader of the free world. It was a position of immense responsibility. With the fall of China, experts in the Defense and State Departments in Washington, D.C., believed that communist expansionism was menacing the security of the entire free world. Fear that the communists, led by the Soviet Union's Stalin, had their eyes on all of Southeast Asia prompted President Truman to approve aid to the French cause. Otherwise, the Americans reasoned, the delicate balance of power which had existed between East and West in the region might very well be upset.

It is important to note, however, that the United States had little interest in helping France preserve its colonial empire. What Truman and the American policymakers *did* want was a Vietnam that would have democratic institutions and be allied with the democracies of the world. This, of course, put the Americans in a sticky position. Unless the United States was willing to send troops to fight in Indochina itself, it had no choice but to support France, even if to a large degree the American and French objectives for the region were opposed.

In other words, the United States would have to walk a kind of tightrope, attempting to assist the French militarily, while at the same time pressuring them into doing what they were extremely reluctant to do: granting Vietnam and the other Indochinese states real independence.

Broadly speaking, the United States became embroiled in the First Indochina War because its stated foreign policy objectives, rightly or wrongly, required it to do so. The core of that policy consisted of the Truman Doctrine and containment of communist expansion.

The Truman Doctrine had been elaborated during the crisis of 1947 when both Greece and Turkey, two vital strategic countries of the free world, had been threatened by communist insurgencies. Responding to that threat, President Truman had pledged U.S. support for "free people who are resisting attempted subjugation by armed minorities or by outside pressures."[2] It was an extremely ambitious pledge, really. Some would say too ambitious, as it seemed to indicate that the United States should actively support *any* government resisting communist encroachment.

Containment was a concept originally developed to guide America's policies and actions toward the Soviet Union. The renowned diplomat George F. Kennan, one of America's greatest experts on the Soviet Union and the originator of the containment idea, argued that the United States policy toward the Soviet Union should be one of "long-term, patient but firm and vigilant containment of Russia's expansive tendencies through . . . the adroit and vigilant application of counterforce. . . ."[3] Such expansion should be countered either by economic and technical assistance or, if need be, by armed force. In the case of the French war, the United States would counter communist expansion with economic assistance.

Today, it is almost impossible to recapture the sense of urgency with which the men in Washington, particularly Secretary of State Dean Acheson, the Joint Chiefs of Staff, and the rest of the Defense Department, monitored the world political scene during these years. For although America had been victorious in World War II, it seemed no time at all before it was embroiled in a new kind of war altogether—a "cold war." This was the term American financier and political adviser Bernard Baruch used to describe the political and diplomatic, rather than military, conflict between the Soviet-led Eastern bloc in Europe and China on the one hand, and the United States and Western Europe on the other. Every move was seen as critical. Lack of resolve, signs of weak will, might easily lead to a crisis. The reality of the cold war made the conflict in Indochina an international war. By late 1949, both East and West had a real stake in its outcome.

In the United States, concern over Asia went beyond the Truman administration. The U.S. Congress approved a mutual defense assistance act which called for the deployment of U.S. military advisers to Asia, if deemed necessary. The National Security Council produced an important paper entitled "Position of the United States with Respect to Asia," which President Truman approved as official policy. The paper proposed that the United States continue to use its influence in Asia to satisfy the demands of the various nationalist movements while at the same time minimizing the strain on the colonial powers who sought to constrain those movements.

It was a perplexing statement. For in fueling the fire of Vietnamese nationalism, America would inevitably increase the strain on the French, who had chosen the ineffectual and unpopular Bao Dai as head of state in Vietnam. Bao Dai had little support among the people, and was more interested in French culture, wine, and women than in governing. Nevertheless, in May 1950, Secretary of State Acheson announced that the United States would begin to send aid directly to the Vietnamese government in the hope of improving the Bao Dai government's image in the eyes of the Vietnamese people.

The Acheson announcement meant that a profoundly important step had been taken. The United States was no longer simply helping its ally France to hold the line against communism in Southeast Asia. It had begun to assume that responsibility itself. Were the French to falter, the United States would be under great pressure to take action. Its prestige was at stake, for if Vietnam fell to the communists after significant direct U.S. aid had been sent in to shore up a democratic regime, America's credibility among the emerging nations would be diminished. According to the "domino theory" accepted by America's foreign-policy makers in the early 1950s, if Vietnam went communist, it would not be long before the rest of Indochina would follow suit.

Over the next four years, until the war ended with the partition of Vietnam at the 17th Parallel, the Americans would provide more than two-thirds of the money required for the French war effort. The first American military advisers went to Vietnam in 1950, setting up MAAG—the Military Assistance Advisory Group.

The Americans, wanting France to move Vietnam toward independence, put pressure on the French to establish a national Vietnamese army. The French reluctantly agreed, but the new army remained a lightly armed, poorly trained token force, largely because the French really didn't want an independent army in Vietnam in the first place.

The French war effort made little headway against a determined enemy. The wily guerrillas continued to evade French and Vietnamese troops, striking only when they could escape French air power and artillery by fleeing into the jungles and mountains.

There was some progress in French pacification efforts by 1953, but the strength and coordination of the Vietminh's political and military cells (small groups of men and women who trained and worked together closely as an inseparable unit) continued to baffle the French. The Vietminh seemed to know France's moves on the battlefield before they even occurred.

In 1953, the Eisenhower administration, increasingly frustrated by France's failure to achieve pacification, insisted that the French install a new commander. The French sent in General Henri Navarre with a fresh plan to eradicate the Vietminh's military forces, which had grown in size and sophistication with a great deal of help from their Chinese allies.

The Navarre plan called for the use of a beefed-up Vietnamese army to pacify the villages. Meanwhile the French expeditionary force would be expanded. Its mission: to hunt down the Vietminh's forces, wherever they were, and to engage and destroy them through concentrated air power and artillery fire. In the summer of 1953, Navarre's plan came tantalizingly close to achieving its objective on several occasions. Whole divisions of the VPA (Vietnamese Peo-

ple's Army) were surrounded, but General Vo Nguyen Giap, the Vietminh's commander in chief, always found a way to break through French lines and bring out his troops with only minor losses.

Frustrated by repeated failures over the summer to crush Giap, Navarre decided to challenge the Vietminh deep in the heart of their own territory, at an outpost in northwestern Vietnam overlooking a valley in Laos. Navarre hoped he could draw Giap's divisions into a major battle in this isolated spot. He occupied it with some of his best troops, including units of the legendary French Foreign Legion. The outpost was situated near the sparsely populated village of Dien Bien Phu.

Unfortunately for the French, Navarre's plan was fatally flawed. The 15,000 men allotted to the task were simply too few to hold their position in the event of a major Vietminh attack. And Navarre, like the Americans who fought after the French left Vietnam, underestimated the enemy and dismissed the possibility of such an attack.

By March 1954 the Vietminh had surrounded the French outpost with 40,000 men, Chinese-supplied siege guns to hammer the French positions, and an impressive array of antiaircraft weapons to prevent the French from air-dropping supplies. It was an astounding feat. Gradually, the Vietminh blew the French outpost to pieces. One by one, after wave upon wave of Vietminh infantry assaults, the French positions collapsed.

By early May, the Vietminh had wiped out the outlying French positions and tunneled in close to the heart of the French forces. On May 7, after launching rocket attacks, Vietminh infantry stormed the outpost for the last time. The French force, what was left of it, surrendered.

With the disastrous defeat at Dien Bien Phu, whatever little will the French politicians and people had to carry on the conflict known in France as the "Dirty War" evaporated. All that was left to do was negotiate a settlement.

Vo Nguyen Giap, the commander of the Vietnamese People's Army, and the man who planned the crucial Dien Bien Phu campaign. (Camera Press Ltd. photo.)

How was it possible that the partnership of two great Western powers, France and the United States, had been unable to crush the Vietminh? The answer to this question, like those to so many other questions concerning warfare in Vietnam, is complicated. Ho Chi Minh had gotten the whole population of the territory he controlled behind the war effort, mobilizing men, women, and even children to defeat French colonialism. The French, despite massive American aid, had failed to instill unity among the numerous sects, private armies, and political factions that had fought against the Vietminh, or more particularly, against its tightly knit communist leadership. American aid had been mismanaged, and the Vietnamese army had never become an effective fighting force, its loyalties split between France and Vietnam. The lack of support for the war at home in France had damaged morale in the field as well.

Although the Americans had financed the war effort, the partnership had been awkward, and at times terribly strained. This was hardly a surprise, since the United States and France had entirely different objectives in Vietnam. The United States could apply some pressure on the French to move toward establishing a truly nationalist, pro-Western government in Vietnam, but if it applied too much pressure, the French might pull out, leaving America as the sole Western power trying to keep Vietnam from going communist. Annoyed by American intrusion into their war, the French resisted American proposals for reform and deliberately refrained from providing U.S. officials with information about the prosecution of the war. All of this led to mistrust, confusion, and bitterness—hardly a prescription for victory.

With the fall of Dien Bien Phu and the end of the Korean War, the great powers met in Geneva, Switzerland, to settle the fate of Vietnam. At first, the Vietminh delegation, headed by Pham Van Dong, a dedicated soldier of communist revolution and later the prime minister of all of Vietnam, refused to talk about a military cease-fire unless it came with a political settlement as well. But the United States and France would have no part of this. In one of the many

French infantry dug in for battle against the Vietminh. (E.C.P. Armées.)

ironies of Vietnamese history, it was the allies of the Vietminh who prevailed upon Pham Van Dong to accept a cease-fire without a true political solution. The Chinese were anxious to appear reasonable to the West, and they also feared that if the agreement established political means for the Vietminh to gain control over all of Vietnam, the United States would have no choice but to send in combat troops.

Reluctantly, Pham Van Dong gave in. The "Final Declaration" of Vietnam partitioned the country at the 17th Parallel. Bao Dai, the last emperor of Vietnam, would head the newly created State of Vietnam in the south, and Ho Chi Minh's Democratic Republic of Vietnam (DRV) would rule the north. Elections were supposed to be held to determine the permanent government of all of Vietnam within two years, and an international commission would supervise those elections.

Unfortunately, this "Final Declaration" marked nothing more than a temporary end to the fighting. Bao Dai denounced the agreement. The United States refused to agree to the election provision, knowing that the Vietminh's superior organizational skills would win them the election. However, the American delegation did agree to "refrain from the threat or use of force to disturb" the agreement. Bedell Smith, an American representative, added that the United States would "view any renewal of the aggression . . . as seriously threatening international peace and security."[4] This meant that the door was kept open for further U.S. involvement in Vietnam. In fact, the Americans had no intention of allowing the communists to gain control over the southern half of the country, no matter how they attempted to get it.

The American commitment to Vietnam, therefore, was based largely on events and ideas unrelated to the realities of the situation in Vietnam itself. The foreign policy experts in Washington were by and large optimistic about their ability to keep the communists out of South Vietnam, because they underestimated the difficulties of establishing and maintaining an effective, popular, and democratic government there. They believed America had the technology and know-how to create a new and more powerful government capable of standing up to the communists who controlled the north.

The truth of the matter was that Vietnamese culture had been shaped by Confucian values, by a reverence and respect for authority and hierarchy above all else. The Confucian tradition, whatever its merits, did not place a high value upon personal liberty, free-

The varied landscape of Vietnam posed immense difficulties for all foreign soldiers who fought there. Here U.S. Navy boats patrol one of the many small rivers in the Mekong Delta in the mid-1960s. (Army News Features, courtesy Shelby L. Stanton.)

dom, or individual rights. There was, in fact, little social basis for democracy in Vietnam, a fact which escaped the notice of the American decision-makers.

Nor did the Americans realize that, however unwittingly, they had cast themselves in the unenviable role of France's replacement, another foreign invading force on Vietnamese soil. In the years that would follow, the communists would strive to portray the Americans as intruders, not democratic liberators. In large measure, they would be successful.

2. An Uneasy Partnership: The United States and Ngo Dinh Diem

On June 26, 1954, a group of people, perhaps several hundred in number, gathered at an airport in Saigon. They were there to welcome the new prime minister of South Vietnam, a man named Ngo Dinh Diem. For the next nine years, Diem would be the central figure in South Vietnamese politics, the man the Americans were counting on to unify the fractured political forces of the new nation.

Diem had been appointed by Bao Dai earlier that month during a visit to the emperor's chateau at Cannes, France. Bao Dai had made the appointment in the belief that Diem was the man who could bring American pressure to bear on the French to leave the country entirely, thereby promoting the cause of true independence.

Could Diem do the job? He certainly had influential friends in the United States. And because he was a well-known anticommunist, chances were good that the Eisenhower administration would look favorably upon him. In the eyes of American foreign policy experts, South Vietnam required not just a good nationalist who would move the country forward politically and economically, but a leader who was strong enough to withstand the challenge from Ho Chi Minh's regime in the north.

Ngo Dinh Diem was born in 1901 in central Vietnam, the third child of well-to-do parents. Active in Vietnamese politics since the 1930s, Diem had served in the government bureaucracy after receiving his degree from the school of public administration in Hanoi. After uncovering a communist plot to stir revolt in 1929, the French appointed him minister of the interior. But Diem soon became dis-

Ngo Dinh Diem waves from a balcony of the presidential palace in Saigon. (AP/Wide World Photos.)

illusioned with the French. When his suggestion that a Vietnamese legislature be invested with real power was turned down, he resigned, and began to travel widely in the hope of gaining influential friends who might be of use to him in the cause of Vietnamese independence. He spent a considerable amount of time in the United States lecturing on Vietnam, gaining access to many influential people in the U.S. government.

Diem's reign over South Vietnam, which lasted until 1963, was a tempestuous one. Historians have criticized his policies as ineffective and wrongheaded, but there is little doubt that he was a true nationalist, not just a figurehead placed at the helm of a puppet country to see that America's wishes for his native country were fulfilled. Even Ho Chi Minh respected Diem's commitment to independence. But Diem could never command the loyalty of the people as Ho Chi Minh did.

As a respected nationalist and fervent anticommunist, Diem was a logical choice to lead South Vietnam. But he was not a born leader. A tireless talker, he could sit for hours, dressed in his white sharkskin suit, reciting detail after detail about his personal experiences, chain-smoking all the while. He was a poor listener, preferring to take advice from those he trusted—usually his brother Nhu or Nhu's wife, the striking Madame Nhu—rather than from those who were most in touch with the wide range of problems his fledgling nation faced. He wanted independence for his people, but he was not willing to go out among them to stir up support. That was not behavior fitting for a head of state.

It was a pity that South Vietnam did not at the time have a leader with Ho's capacity and talent for leadership, because the task at hand was truly a daunting one. What existed in the country at this time, as Frances Fitzgerald has written in her book *Fire in the Lake*, was a "political jungle of warlords, sects, bandits, partisan troops, and secret societies."[1] The most prominent and powerful groups Diem would have to wrestle power from were the religious sects and the Binh Xuyen, a crime syndicate with an army of well over 20,000 men. To make matters even more complicated, the French, who still maintained a presence in the country, did all that they could to discredit the new head of state and his American supporters.

In the summer of 1954, the South Vietnamese army's chief of staff, French-educated Nguyen Van Hinh, called openly for the removal of Diem, and with other officers he plotted a *coup d'etat*. Had it not been for the help of Edward Lansdale, an American CIA operative, Diem might not have lasted through one year in office. Lansdale was in charge of a number of covert operations in these early years, including efforts to upset the transportation network in Hanoi and to gather intelligence in North Vietnam. The American had tricked some of Hinh's fellow plotters into taking a trip to Manila to get them out of the way, and he had used CIA money to bribe sect members into supporting the prime minister.

Lansdale's maneuverings hardly put an end to the political infighting in Saigon. In April 1955, the Binh Xuyen and the two major religious sects joined together to challenge Diem's control. When Diem refused to share political power, the challengers tried force. In late April, the streets of Saigon were ablaze with small-arms, artillery, and mortar fire as the sects and the Binh Xuyen fought Diem's troops. Within a month, to the surprise of many, including some Americans on the scene, the opposition had folded.

The resounding success of Diem's forces heartened the anxious men in Washington, especially Secretary of State John Foster Dulles, who was a firm believer in U.S. support for the regime. Lansdale weighed in with his judgment, claiming that the unsuccessful coup showed Diem was a strong leader, a man who could be counted on and who had the loyalty of the army. American support for Diem after the episode also forced a confrontation between the United States and France about the leadership of the country. Ultimately, France decided to pull the remainder of its troops out of Vietnam rather than support Diem. One of the many players in the political turmoil of South Vietnam was now out of the picture.

Five months after the defeat of the sects and the Binh Xuyen, an election was held pitting Bao Dai against Diem. Diem, enjoying more American aid than ever before, easily won the election, gaining a suspiciously high percentage of the popular vote.

Diem had secured power, but in a very real way, his troubles had just begun. Survival of the young South Vietnamese state would depend upon the creation of a strong, highly motivated army. Diem's tendency to appoint cronies of his family to top army posts demoralized the officer corps. Many of these appointees seemed more French than Vietnamese in their bearing and outlook, which made it especially hard for them to gain the respect of troops drawn from the peasantry. Corruption in the army, as in the government itself, was rampant. A good deal of American military aid ended up being sold on the black market.

Diem's obsession with secrecy and personal loyalty also caused difficulties. Along with his brothers—all of whom occupied important governmental positions—he controlled a secret political society which challenged the regular chain of command in the armed forces.

But despite these problems, the Eisenhower administration, like the Kennedy and Johnson administrations which followed, preferred to view the delicate situation in Vietnam optimistically. There were those in government who even referred to the leader of South Vietnam as "the savior of Southeast Asia." Calling Diem this, of course, was a wild exaggeration, but it had a purpose. For the administration knew how important it was that Diem's own people believe he was capable of uniting the sundry political factions of the nation and steering the nation toward a better life, a life that would allow them some say in their own destiny. The alternative seemed to the administration in Washington, and indeed to many Vietnamese nationalists, nightmarish: a Vietnam unified by force, whose direction came not from the people but from a small coterie of dedicated revolutionaries in Hanoi, Beijing, and Moscow. By exalting Diem's limited achievements, Eisenhower hoped to rally both Americans and Vietnamese to the cause of a free, pro-Western South Vietnam.

A U.S. adviser, Army captain Linton Beasley, shows South Vietnamese troops how to use the Thompson submachine gun (foreground) and the M-1 carbine (far left). Even in the early 1960s, many South Vietnamese units were equipped with World War II—vintage weapons like these. (U.S. Army photo.)

The decision to give full support to Diem wasn't solely President Eisenhower's. A majority of the U.S. Congress supported the decision. It is not hard to see why. With the defeat of the French in the First Indochina War, America's policymakers were more determined than ever to maintain a pro-Western South Vietnam. No one familiar with the situation in Vietnam honestly believed that Diem or any other South Vietnamese leader could go it alone. If South Vietnam went communist, how long would it be before Laos, Cambodia, and other Southeast Asian nations followed? North Vietnam and China had already been lost.

So it was that the American crusade against communist expansion picked up momentum. It was an immense challenge, and in the memos and documents of the key American players there is a sense of the excitement and urgency they felt as they sized up the numerous tasks which stood before them. The objective of U.S. policy in Vietnam during this period went far beyond simply supplying money to a foreign government. Our expertise and technological resources would be brought into play to transform Vietnam into a model country, with enlightened institutions and a prosperous people. George Herring neatly summarized American thinking about Vietnam when he wrote in *America's Longest War* that Vietnam became "a testing ground for the viability of American ideology and institutions."[2]

Social, economic, and agricultural development teams were flown in to assess the situation. They produced thousands of pages of recommendations on how to improve productivity and modernize the country's economy, transportation network, and political institutions.

In 1955 alone, the United States pumped $355 million in military and political aid into South Vietnam. To shore up security in the villages, a team from Michigan State University's School of Police Administration was brought in. They developed a rural police force, something which had never existed before. The Americans believed such a force would curb the progress of communist propaganda cadres already operating in South Vietnam.

U.S. dollars were used to pay the salaries of South Vietnamese government employees. Social scientists and foreign service officers trained Vietnamese in the ways of Western democratic government, while engineers designed and executed projects to improve the country's roads, airports, and harbors.

No task was more ambitious or more challenging than the creation of an effective army. In 1956 the Military Assistance and Advisory Group (MAAG) took this task over from the French. U.S. advisers under the command of U.S. Army General Samuel Williams attempted to mold the ARVN (Army of the Republic of Vietnam) into a professional organization, dedicated to protecting the people and their government.

It wouldn't be easy. The French had taken most of the modern military equipment with them when they left. The Vietnamese had few military specialists—engineers, mechanics, logistics people (supply specialists), or artillerymen. The lack of a common language hampered communication between adviser and trainee and made it difficult to establish trust. Many Vietnamese wondered if the Americans were just another colonial power out to exploit them under the guise of offering help.

The effort to locate and root out the communists operating in South Vietnam during this time did not progress as smoothly as either Diem or the Eisenhower administration wished. One cause of problems appears to have been intelligence gathering, crucial to the success of all military operations. The reports of the American advisors are filled with complaints about the inaccuracy of the South Vietnamese army's information. Those who were familiar with the South Vietnamese intelligence network at the time saw it as a tangled web without a clear hierarchy or organization. "The Central Intelligence Agency," reports Ronald Spector in his book on the early years of the U.S. Army's involvement in Vietnam, *Advice and Support*, "knew of no less than six major and several other, lesser groups competing with one another for information."[3]

The problems, however, did not reside solely with the South Vietnamese. American bureaucracy, the sheer number of agencies and organizations, worked against the American effort to build a strong nation in South Vietnam. We will see numerous examples of this throughout the story of the Vietnam War. In the 1950s and early 1960s, for instance, the U.S. Army and the CIA worked frequently at cross-purposes.

Bureaucracy also lay behind the excessive optimism about the progress the American advisory effort was making in general. The head of the Combat Arms Training Organization, reflecting on

meetings to assess progress held by General Williams, said that "in a number of cases people held back a little in reporting anything wrong because they feared that it would reflect on them adversely."[4] A common fear among the Americans in Vietnam was that if the reports were not optimistic, another organization or agency might be assigned to the job. And that was bad for one's career.

The army of South Vietnam had to be strong if the communists were to be prevented from achieving their objective of gaining complete control over the South Vietnamese population. A strong army alone, though, would not ensure the loyalty and support of the people. Prosperity would. Accordingly, Diem's government set about the task of land reform. Ever since the French had been in Vietnam, wealthy landlords had placed a harsh burden upon the peasantry, taking a high proportion of their crops as rent and driving many peasants into debt. Diem's land reform called for limiting any one landlord's holdings to 267 acres. The government would buy the remainder, and then sell it at low cost to those Vietnamese who had no land.

But the administration of the land reform program, carried out under American direction, was cumbersome and ineffective. Corrupt officials cheated peasants at every turn. In some provinces, it took several years for the officials even to initiate the reforms.

In 1959, when it was apparent to all that the reform program was foundering, Diem announced the *agroville* program. The *agrovilles* were to be fortified, secure villages, built more or less from scratch in areas in the countryside where loyalty to the government was weak or absent. In some cases, the *agrovilles* would be situated in areas known to be under the control of the communists, or Vietcong, as the South Vietnamese were now beginning to call them. These fortified villages were to be patrolled by local civil defense and police forces, which were in the process of being formed. The idea was simple: to prevent communists and other antigovernment forces from disrupting the life of the South Vietnamese people.

The *agroville* program was an outright failure. The Vietnamese

An ARVN medic tries to save the life of a wounded Vietcong soldier. The soldier's wife, who appeared shortly after the firefight, looks anxiously on. (U.S. Army photo.)

An ARVN soldier destroys captured Vietcong propaganda after a raid in the Camau Peninsula, the southernmost part of South Vietnam. (U.S. Army photo.)

have an extraordinary attachment to their ancestral land, and they resented being forced to move to these semimilitary outposts. Bitterness and resentment grew deeper when the resettled peasants learned that they themselves would be forced to build the villages. Because of resentment, sabotage, and corruption, only twenty-two *agrovilles* were built before the project was abandoned. It later was revealed that the officer in charge of the program was in fact a communist agent determined to use his position to turn the peasantry against Diem's government.

While Diem and his American allies were struggling to create a strong and unified South Vietnam, Ho Chi Minh's forces in the north were gathering strength and forging strategy for a new war. Eight years of war against the French had left them incapable of launching an all-out invasion, at least for a while. So in the first few years after Geneva, the communists pursued a strategy focused upon "political struggle." While North Vietnam rebuilt from the First Indochina War, it would send its propaganda agents south to join those cadres (tightly knit, small groups of trained communists) which had been left behind to foment revolution.

The goal of political struggle (as distinct from overt armed struggle) was to turn the people in the south against Diem and the United States, and toward communist revolution. Political struggle took place within the borders of North Vietnam, too. The communist leadership, borrowing techniques from Communist China, attempted to rid North Vietnam of its "corrupt elements," the landlords and unbelievers. Society would be redesigned according to the dictates of communist theory. Cadres were sent into villages to gather evidence against those who did not fall into line. People's courts were created. It was expected that each village would produce a certain number of guilty parties. Fearing the worst if those quotas were not met, the people's courts imprisoned or killed many innocents. Executions without trials were commonplace.

Political struggle was far more successful in North Vietnam than it was in the south. In South Vietnam, Diem's anticommunist campaign had succeeded in uncovering many of those sympathetic to the communist cause. These men and women were either executed or imprisoned. Recognizing that despite Diem's various failures their revolution was losing ground, the communist cadres in the south pleaded for help from their North Vietnamese comrades. At the urging of Le Duan, the influential secretary of the Lao Dong, or Workers Party (as the Vietnamese Communist Party was now called), in late 1957 the use of *limited* armed struggle began. "Limited armed struggle" meant subversion through terrorist tactics rather than all-out war. Vietcong insurgents, mainly native southerners, were sent back to their homeland via Laos by truck. They then traveled on foot—sometimes hundreds of miles in the provinces of the Mekong Delta—to join forces with their beleaguered comrades.

Throughout the late 1950s the communists exerted more and more pressure on the South Vietnamese government, testing its will and the ability of the American-supported regime to withstand attacks. In May 1959, word came down from Hanoi to the southern cadres that it was time for even more aggressive tactics. Thereafter, assassinations of village chiefs unsympathetic to the revolution and of minor government officials occurred with alarming frequency. Many known innocents, people with no connection to the Diem government, were harassed by the Vietcong in order to demonstrate that Diem's security forces were unable to protect the villages and to discredit the government in the eyes of the people. In 1959, more than 1,000 government officials were killed. In 1961, the toll was reported to be around 4,000.

In addition, highly trained military units began to attack South Vietnamese military installations. The attacks were most frequent in the western Mekong Delta, where the dense jungles and rugged terrain provided excellent cover for the lightly armed Vietcong.

On July 8, 1959, some American soldiers were enjoying themselves inside the MAAG compound at Bien Hoa, about twenty-five miles northeast of Saigon. They were watching a movie along with a few South Vietnamese soldiers in the mess hall. When the first reel of film ended, Master Sergeant Chester Ovnand got up and switched on the light to change the reel. As soon as the light went on, Vietcong guerrillas began firing their submachine guns through the windows, killing Ovnand, Major Dale Buis, two South Vietnamese soldiers, and an eight-year-old boy before fleeing into the darkness. Buis and Ovnand are considered the first Americans to die in the Vietnam War.

By January 1960, the Vietcong—by now often called the VC— were conducting military operations on a previously unheard-of scale. On January 26, 200 men attacked an ARVN regiment at Trang Sup. They destroyed a number of buildings and made off with a cache of rifles, pistols, and machine guns. The attack greatly embarrassed the

ARVN brass. Soon thereafter, the MAAG commander, General Williams, conferred with Diem about the pressing need to reform the ARVN in order to make it a better-organized fighting force. The president of South Vietnam promised to implement reforms in the army and also to check corruption in the government.

But little or no action was taken. The American ambassador to South Vietnam, Elbridge Durbrow, cabled Washington that Diem refused to say specifically what he was going to do to improve the performance of his army and his government. The more pressure U.S. officials applied, the more President Diem seemed to retreat into his palace, talking to no one but his brother Nhu, the head of South Vietnam's secret police.

In the waning days of the Eisenhower administration, the war against the Vietcong seemed to be going in the wrong direction, even though the government of South Vietnam had received more than $1 billion in aid since 1955. In January 1961, John Fitzgerald Kennedy assumed the presidency of the United States. The strikingly handsome former senator from Massachusetts had a strong commitment to the preservation of free institutions and governments around the world. To the men Kennedy brought with him to Washington as advisers, many of whom were well known in the academic and business worlds, the defense of democratic institutions had never been so important for American national security.

Looking back at the cold war of the late 1950s and early 1960s, it is not hard to see why Kennedy was so determined to show resolve in the struggle between East and West. For this was a period when the Soviet Union was particularly aggressive and intent on embarrassing the United States. The old colonies of the European powers were now new nations, and the struggle between the democratic and communist worlds for control and influence intensified. New, more powerful nuclear weapons threatened an already fragile peace. In January 1961, Premier Khrushchev of the Soviet Union delivered an ominous speech in which he pledged support for all wars of "na-

The village of Tan Khai, destroyed by the Vietcong. (Courtesy Shelby L. Stanton.)

tional liberation." There was talk about closing off West Berlin to the West, and the Soviet Union increased its aid to Cuba and to communist insurgents in Laos, Vietnam's neighbor.

Convinced that the East-West struggle was to be waged in the newly emerging nations of the so-called third world (nations aligned with neither East nor West) and that Vietnam was the "cornerstone of the free world in Southeast Asia," Kennedy had no intention of permitting a communist takeover. "South Vietnam," writes George C. Herring in *America's Longest War*, "would become a test case of America's determination to uphold its commitments in a menacing world and of its capacity to meet the new challenges posed by guerrilla warfare in the emerging nations. Thus Kennedy was even less willing than Truman and Eisenhower to permit the fall of Vietnam to Communism."[5]

It was concern over communist success in the emerging nations that led Kennedy to consider a new military doctrine called "counterinsurgency." The doctrine, which the United States continued to emphasize throughout the Vietnam War, was that the main objective of the military should not be the destruction of the enemy's armed forces, but the winning of the allegiance of the people by directly challenging communist control of the villages and providing a wealth of medical and technical assistance. Accordingly, the president put a new emphasis upon counterinsurgency training in the armed forces with a view toward "winning the hearts and minds" of the people of South Vietnam.

By the fall of 1961, President Kennedy, alarmed at the deteriorating situation on the ground in Vietnam, sent General Maxwell Taylor and an entire planeload of military and political advisers to Vietnam to assess the situation there firsthand and report on what they found. The Taylor delegation arrived in Saigon at a moment of crisis. The insurgents' attacks west of the city had increased, and flooding had destroyed much of the rice crop, driving the price of this precious commodity way up. President Diem had declared a national state of emergency.

All of this set the tone for Taylor's report to Kennedy. South Vietnam, the general reported, was in big trouble. The government needed additional U.S. help, and fast. If the communist threat was to be averted, it would take not only more aid and more advisers, but U.S. combat troops.

Not all of the president's advisers accepted Taylor's assessment, however. George Ball, one of the most astute, feared that sending in a limited number of American troops wouldn't solve problems that were, after all, the result of both external aggression and internal instability. If the United States sent in the 8,000 troops Taylor thought necessary for the job, the gateway would be open for perhaps hundreds of thousands of U.S. soldiers to follow.

Three top-ranking American officials in South Vietnam: left to right, General Paul D. Harkins, commander, Military Assistance Command, Vietnam; Admiral Harry D. Felt, CINCPAC commander; and U.S. ambassador to South Vietnam Fredrick E. Nolting. (U.S. Army photo.)

Sterling Cottrell, an official in the State Department, pointed out that the war was being fought in the villages, and foreign troops, with their lack of knowledge of Vietnamese traditions, customs, and language, wouldn't be very effective in that kind of war. American troops wouldn't change the fact that the South Vietnamese army remained unpopular, or that many who had initially supported Diem were no longer sure he would be able to pull the country together. Cottrell came right out and said it would be a mistake for America "to commit itself irrevocably to the defeat of the Communists."[6]

After listening to the opposing arguments, Kennedy did what American presidents had previously done when decisions had to be made about Vietnam. He compromised. He refused to send combat troops, but he agreed to send more money. Helicopters would be shipped along with more advisers. At the time of Taylor's mission to Vietnam, the United States had about 3,000 advisers in the country. Within two years the number would climb to 16,000.

In 1962, despite the ever-increasing flow of aid and advisers, the situation continued to deteriorate. All over South Vietnam, government installations and ARVN posts were attacked. There were some influential members of the U.S. State Department who favored cutting economic and military aid to Vietnam altogether. But by this time, such a drastic turnaround was not really an option for President Kennedy. Diem, and, indeed, most observers of the scene, knew that the prestige of the United States was clearly on the line in Vietnam. This gave Diem some leverage of his own. He pressed the Americans for more help, for more advisers and helicopters and pilots, and he got them. American soldiers were now going out in small numbers on patrol with ARVN units. Although the Kennedy administration downplayed the escalation of the U.S. role with the press, American advisers were now fighting and dying in Vietnam.

By the summer of 1963, Diem's regime was fast approaching yet another crisis. His intransigence and consistent refusal to undertake reforms had alienated many in Washington and Saigon, the Vietcong were on the move, and ARVN generals, always active in the political machinations of the country, were plotting *coups d'état*. A number of these generals, led by Duong Van "Big" Minh, were in constant contact with CIA operative Lucien Conein, one of the more experienced and colorful players in the drama that was about to unfold. They had contacted Conein to find out what the United States would do if they were to overthrow President Diem.

As fall approached, things grew worse for the president of South Vietnam. The Buddhists, of whom there were a substantial number in South Vietnam, resented Diem's favoritism toward the Catholics. When the Buddhists took to the streets in protest, Diem's police broke up the gatherings, on a number of occasions using brutal force.

On June 11, 1963, in Saigon, Quang Duc, a sixty-six-year-old Buddhist monk, drenched his body in gasoline, knelt down in a position of prayer, and set himself ablaze, commiting suicide as an act of protest. The pictures of Quang Duc were published in newspapers worldwide, setting off a furor of protest. The American ambassador at the time, the stately Henry Cabot Lodge, warned Diem that repression must cease if U.S. aid was to continue.

Villagers look on as a Montagnard commando and an American Special Forces officer search for the enemy. The Montagnards, the people of the central highlands of South Vietnam, were recruited and trained by the Green Berets to fight the Vietcong. (U.S. Army photo.)

The repression did not cease, and turmoil spread throughout South Vietnam—just what Big Minh and the other generals needed to get their coup off the ground. The details of the plot remain obscure, but it appears that at one point in late October, Ambassador Lodge indicated to the generals that the United States would not stand in the way of an attempted coup. After several months of secret planning, the generals were sure they had the necessary support in the army to carry out the takeover successfully. General Tran Van Don, another key figure in the plot, had kept in close contact with Conein as the delicate details were worked out.

On November 1, the rebel troops surrounded the presidential palace. After several hours of fruitless negotiation, Diem and his closest associate, his brother Nhu, slipped out of the palace undetected and fled to a retreat in Cholon, the Chinese district just outside of Saigon.

After realizing that the United States was in no hurry to come to his aid, Diem surrendered upon the condition that the generals guarantee his safety. The generals told him that both he and his brother would be protected. But when the armored personnel carrier sent to retrieve Diem got back to headquarters in Saigon, it contained the bullet-ridden corpses of Diem and his brother.

A few of Diem's ardent supporters in Washington felt that America had betrayed the leader it had installed and propped up for nine years. Most of the policymakers in the Kennedy administration were deeply disturbed at the turn of events, but relieved that Diem was no longer in control. Perhaps now a real leader might be found, a cooperative partner in the struggle to keep South Vietnam free from communism.

Three weeks after Diem was killed, President Kennedy became the victim of an assassin's bullet, and all America was in mourning. Now the leadership of the free world would be in the hands of Kennedy's vice president, a Texan named Lyndon Baines Johnson. And it would be up to LBJ to guide the enigmatic American crusade in South Vietnam.

3. To Bear Any Burden

While the nation mourned the death of a president who had captured the hearts of so many, Lyndon Baines Johnson found himself thrust into the position he had coveted for all of his political life. *He* was now leader of the free world—the thirty-sixth president of the United States. It was the fulfillment of a dream, realized under the worst of circumstances.

LBJ had grown up in the poor hill country of southeastern Texas. From the very beginning, Johnson loved the world of politics, power, and wheeling and dealing. Promising to bring the people of his district electrical power for the first time, he was elected to the House of Representatives in 1938. Within ten years, his oratorical flair, common sense, and ability to get along with people landed him in the U.S. Senate. His abilities were quickly recognized there by the Democratic leaders, and he rose to the position of Senate majority leader in 1953.

Although John Kennedy didn't have strong personal connections to the Texan, Johnson's impressive skills as a dealmaker and legislator made him an excellent choice for vice president.

Johnson believed wholeheartedly in America and the American dream—and he believed he was the right man to bring America peace and prosperity, even if he had to frighten people into moving toward progress *his* way. Johnson's passion was to make the United States a better place, with greater economic opportunities, to be sure, but more important than that, with truly equal justice under the law— equal justice even for black sharecroppers in Mississippi and for minorities in the ghettoes of America's biggest cities. The U.S. govern-

Lyndon Baines Johnson, the first American president to order U.S. combat troops into action in Vietnam. (U.S. Navy photo.)

ment had a responsibility to ensure social justice and equal treatment of everyone. Johnson's vision of America and the specific legislation he proposed to make that vision come alive came to be known as the Great Society program.

Soon after taking the oath of office in Air Force One with a shocked Jacqueline Kennedy standing by his side, Johnson got the first hints that something very ominous stood in the way of the Great Society. The obstacle, of course, was the war in Vietnam. It was not a war he had any great enthusiasm for fighting. And yet as time went on, he became obsessed with the conflict. His greatest fear was that if he cut the American commitment to South Vietnam, he would be labeled the first American president in history to lose a war.

The idea that the greatest free nation in the world lacked the resolve to crush communist aggression—even if that aggression took place 9,000 miles from Washington, D.C.—was inconceivable for a man like Johnson, who had an abiding faith not only in his nation and its ideals, but in himself and his leadership abilities. Lyndon Johnson believed, like so many of the statesmen who came of age after World War II, that if you shrank from resisting aggression, nothing but more aggression would follow. He remembered the infamous Munich agreement, in which the British acquiesced to German annexation of a part of Czechoslovakia. That concession had led to the greatest and most destructive war in history.

While LBJ was an acknowledged master of the art of American politics, he had little experience in foreign affairs. Johnson was used to making deals with the senator from Minnesota or Alabama, or getting on the phone and using his influence with important congressmen to make sure that an important piece of legislation was passed, but he was by all accounts uncomfortable with foreigners and their customs.

When he had gone to Vietnam as President Kennedy's emissary, he'd found it difficult to comprehend the Vietnamese. Nor were the Vietnamese comfortable with Johnson's loud and brash style. There is a kind of directness in the way Americans approach problems that the Vietnamese, with their concern for avoiding conflict and preserving face, find jarring. It is this directness that Johnson exemplified. The subtleties of the Vietnamese character, it might be said, did not easily mesh with the president's rough-edged, down-home approach to power and politics.

The situation in Vietnam when Johnson assumed the presidency was far more grave than it had been at the time of Kennedy's election. The assassination of Diem signaled a new phase in the political turmoil of South Vietnam. The junta of generals who assumed power, all French-educated with little political experience and no close ties to the people, hardly seemed equal to the task at hand: to wipe out the corruption in the army, to organize the people behind the government, and most of all, to defeat the Vietcong, who *were* well organized and quite capable of exploiting the chaotic political situation in Saigon.

Immediately following the downfall of Diem and Nhu, the true extent of Vietcong control over the territory and people of South Vietnam became more apparent to the Americans. It was not a pleasant picture for President Johnson and for the key foreign policy decision-makers he had kept on from the Kennedy administration: the secretary of defense, Robert McNamara, formerly head of the Ford Motor Company; the brilliant—some said coolly arrogant—national security adviser, McGeorge Bundy; and the self-effacing secretary of state, Dean Rusk.

McNamara warned Johnson in late December that unless things changed quickly, South Vietnam could fall. The South Vietnamese were not the sole contributors to the mess. On returning from one of his many fact-finding missions, McNamara claimed that the American team in Vietnam lacked leadership and coordination.

But what could be done about the steadily deteriorating situation in the Saigon political universe, and more important, in the countryside, where the VC were rapidly making progress?

It would not be too long before Johnson would make a major decision, but early 1964 was not the right time, for political rea-

Secretary of Defense Robert S. McNamara, center, with two South Vietnamese officers, on one of his many trips to Vietnam. (U.S. Army photo.)

sons—he feared a markedly increased U.S. commitment in Vietnam would endanger his chances of winning the upcoming presidential election. Instead of sending in U.S. combat troops or some other drastic action, he opted to continue Kennedy's counterinsurgency program by sending in more advisers and aid to strengthen South Vietnamese security. In addition to this, LBJ approved parts of a plan drawn up by Marine General Victor Krulak, calling for the United States to finance a covert war against the North Vietnamese. There would be coastal raids, propaganda leaflets would be dropped, and infiltration of communist troops into South Vietnam from the north would be closely monitored.

Meanwhile, perhaps out of a belief that military solutions are always quicker than political ones, Johnson seemed to dismiss the advice of those foreign policy experts who had voiced the opinion that Vietnam wasn't going to be won by military means alone, that it was a people's war with complex political objectives.

The president appointed a square-jawed paratrooper named William Westmoreland to be U.S. military commander in Vietnam, and as ambassador he chose Maxwell Taylor, a scholar-general whom Kennedy had been fond of. By June 1964, Saigon and the whole countryside were teeming with Americans from scores of agencies, but still there was little progress. The Civilian Irregular Defense Group, composed of both CIA staff and U.S. Army Special Forces advisers, had performed valiantly in their efforts to train local security forces in the remote hinterlands of Vietnam. But the local troops, mostly tribesmen from the central highlands, lacked discipline and commitment. Throughout the war they were outclassed by the enemy.

As the advisers and policymakers carried on their work into the summer, a pivotal event was about to unfold that would change the complexion of the Vietnam War for America. Under OPLAN 34-A, the U.S. Navy's crack commando unit, known as the Seals, had been for some time training South Vietnamese forces to conduct commando raids along the Gulf of Tonkin. If, in fact, the war were to escalate, it would be imperative that the United States and South Vietnam have a clear idea of the kind of defenses that North Vietnam had installed against both bombing from the air and invasion from the sea.

Ambassador Maxwell D. Taylor, visiting the hamlet of My Hao, about twenty miles north of Saigon. Taylor was a key adviser to both the Kennedy and Johnson administrations. (U.S. Army photo.)

By July 1964, the Navy's activities had gone beyond simply training the South Vietnamese. Admiral U. S. Grant Sharp, Commander in Chief, Pacific Command (CINCPAC) and therefore the military officer responsible for overall buildup of American forces in Vietnam, ordered the Seventh Fleet to dispatch the aircraft carrier USS *Ticonderoga*, one of the most powerful symbols of U.S. military might, to the Gulf of Tonkin to provide support for operations in the area. Part of the intelligence-gathering task was going to be dangerous, and there is nothing so comforting to naval commanders as air power. The destroyer USS *Maddox* at this time was assigned the task of sailing in close to the North Vietnamese coast in order to conduct electronic eavesdropping operations. The *Maddox* could pick up sensitive radar signals from the North Vietnamese and would trasmit those signals back to the Philippines and from there to Washington.

The commander of the *Maddox*, Captain Herrick, upon sighting a large number of North Vietnamese sailboats on August 2, realized that he had been detected. Not wanting to engage in hostile action, he asked the Seventh Fleet commander if he could turn the *Maddox* south, away from the North Vietnamese coast. He was ordered at this point to continue sailing north.

When the *Maddox* was within ten miles of the Red River Delta a few hours later, the captain spotted three North Vietnamese PT boats coming toward him on the horizon. The American ship changed course to flee—it wasn't there to do battle—but the faster PT boats began to close in on her. Within minutes, all three North Vietnamese boats had fired torpedoes at the *Maddox*. All missed. It wasn't long before the jets aboard the *Ticonderoga* were airborne and on the scene. The jets sank one boat and severely damaged the other two.

This, the first so-called Tonkin Gulf incident, prompted President Johnson and the Joint Chiefs of Staff, by this time frustrated by the bewildering variety of restraints placed upon U.S. action in Vietnam, to order the Navy to continue patrolling the waters.

Special Forces adviser Sergeant Howard Stevens briefing his Montagnard strike force. (U.S. Army photo.)

On August 4, the *Maddox*, along with another destroyer, the *C. Turner Joy*, returned to the area of the previous attack. The Joint Chiefs put U.S. troops in Asia on alert, fearing wider action. Thunderstorms limited the visibility of the two ships as they approached the coast. Soon, the jittery crews aboard the destroyers were again firing into the night, unsure of what their target was, or where it was.

To this day, no historian has found any conclusive evidence of a North Vietnamese attack. But once the initial reports of the second incident reached Washington, President Johnson was ready to act. He sent jets from two aircraft carriers to bomb North Vietnamese PT boat installations on the coast.

On television that evening, LBJ told the American people that U.S. forces would respond with air attacks against North Vietnam. The Gulf of Tonkin incidents gave President Johnson and his closest advisers what they had wanted: a chance to obtain from Congress a resolution giving them a free hand to respond to developments in Vietnam. In brief, the Tonkin Gulf Resolution authorized the president to take "all necessary measures" to repel an armed attack on U.S. forces and to "prevent further aggression." It also authorized the president to assist any nation that required aid in defense of its freedom.

The resolution, brought before the Senate, was challenged by Senators Wayne Morse and Ernest Gruening, who believed that Congress alone had the right to declare war. Surely the Tonkin Gulf Resolution had the effect of transferring that power to the president. This argument, however, fell upon deaf ears. Congress, having supported one aid package after another to save Vietnam, was not willing to withdraw its support from the president in a crisis. The resolution passed overwhelmingly.

The American people, too, swept up in the excitement of the moment, approved of the president's resolution and his swift reply to aggression. Communist China and the Soviet Union, not surprisingly, felt differently. They pledged further support to North Vietnam, describing that country not as an aggressor but as a victim of U.S. imperialism. Soon after the incident, U.S. intelligence reported that North Vietnamese runways were being expanded to accommodate jet fighters.

The Gulf of Tonkin story made headlines around the world. Throughout late 1964 and early 1965, both sides in the conflict pressed hard in the propaganda war, each trying to portray the opposing party as the aggressor, the side hungry for war.

It was vital to the government of the United States that its European allies interpret the conflict in Vietnam as a test of Western democracy's character and will to resist encroachment from communism. For their part, the North Vietnamese called the American

Following the death of her husband, this woman helped defend a village from a VC assault by passing ammunition to soldiers. She was awarded the Vietnamese Cross of Gallantry for her efforts. (U.S. Army photo.)

bombing of their territory criminal, an unjust act by a country that had no business in Vietnam in the first place. The North Vietnamese simply denied that they were sending large numbers of troops down the Ho Chi Minh Trail—which by this point they were doing—and claimed that their role was restricted to helping the southern insurgency with guns and other supplies.

Meanwhile, the situation on the ground in late 1964 grew worse. In the critical Mekong Delta region, not very far from Saigon itself, the VC were no longer applying hit-and-run tactics. Now they were staying put and fighting. The communists were challenging the ARVN and Green Beret–trained irregular forces that were supposed to provide security in rural areas—and they were winning.

Not long after the Tonkin Gulf incident, Saigon was in a state of near anarchy, as Catholics and Buddhists battled each other in the streets. Prime Minister Nguyen Khanh (who had replaced the junta that had overthrown Diem) was unable to restore order, and under great pressure from Saigon's student population to effect reforms, he resigned. On November 1, 1964, a daring Vietcong raid on the American air base at Bien Hoa resulted in five American deaths and twenty damaged aircraft. Bien Hoa was only twelve miles from Saigon. The attack stunned the allied forces and reinforced the notion in Washington that something major had to be done to improve security.

This Vietnamese peasant casts a stoic eye upon the ruins of her village, which was burned down by Vietcong guerrillas on July 12, 1964. (U.S. Army photo.)

And so it was. The United States would initiate a major bombing campaign against North Vietnam.

The bombing was to be done in two phases. First, there would be limited raids along the Ho Chi Minh Trail in Laos to reduce the capacity of the Vietcong to carry the fight to the South Vietnamese. The second phase would be a more intensive campaign directed against North Vietnam itself. This second phase, however, wouldn't be implemented until improvement had been made in the political affairs of South Vietnam. In other words, it would be presented to South Vietnam's leaders as a reward for restoring political stability.

Unfortunately, the political situation continued to deteriorate. Vice Air Marshal Nguyen Cao Ky and General Nguyen Van Thieu, the two men who emerged as South Vietnam's leaders at this time, either could not or would not try to pacify the Buddhists, who con-

Following the example of Buddhist monk Quang Duc, who committed suicide by fire in 1963, numerous Buddhists protested government persecution by publicly burning themselves. (Wide World Photos.)

The beach at Da Nang on March 8, 1965. The U.S. Marines have landed. (U.S. Marine Corps photo.)

tinued to protest against their unjust treatment. Fiery suicides persisted, and there were angry anti-American demonstrations calling for the resignation of Ambassador Taylor. After a VC raid against the American base at Pleiku, in which nine soldiers were killed and five aircraft destroyed, the U.S. Air Force initiated Operation Flaming Dart. U.S. pilots attacked and severely damaged several North Vietnamese military bases in the southern panhandle of North Vietnam, just above the 17th Parallel.

The Vietcong, lacking any air force of their own, responded with more attacks on U.S. air bases. The inability of the ARVN to protect those bases effectively led General William Westmoreland to ask President Johnson for U.S. Marines to provide security. The president approved the request.

On March 8, 1965, the first American combat units arrived on the beach at Da Nang. The landing of the marines hardly caused a stir back in the United States. LBJ had presented their arrival as a temporary measure. As soon as security could be handled by the South Vietnamese, the marines would be removed. In reality, however, the introduction of marines radically altered the level of American involvement in Vietnam. With combat troops in the country, the incentive to escalate—to add more troops should problems continue to plague South Vietnam—was higher than ever. By June it leaked to the press that American troops in Vietnam had received permission to conduct offensive operations. Johnson, like President Nixon, who followed after him, sought to hide the real nature of the involvement from the American people, fearing dissent, and hoping, perhaps foolishly, that the stay of American ground troops would be short.

Soon after the U.S. Marines went ashore at Da Nang, in response to requests from General Westmoreland, Johnson authorized the deployment of 40,000 additional ground combat troops to Vietnam. The air war, too, would be expanded. In April, 3,600 sorties (a sortie is one flight of one plane) were flown against North Vietnam. With troops already committed to Southeast Asia, Johnson turned to Congress, asking for more funds, $700 million, for military purposes in Vietnam. Congress granted the request.

Debate continued among the senior foreign policy advisers, but momentum was clearly on the side of escalation in Vietnam. As the summer wore on, Westmoreland and the Joint Chiefs asked for more than 150,000 additional troops and permission to shift to a more offensive posture. The North Vietnamese, after all, hardly seemed daunted by the limited measures that Washington had taken to save its ally. They were more than capable of counter-escalating.

By July 1965, according to a formerly classified memo from McGeorge Bundy to the president, there were 75,000 combat troops in Vietnam. However, 75,000 troops, even with the awesome firepower at their disposal, couldn't reverse the considerable momen-

Soldiers of the First Infantry Division move off their landing zone in search of the Vietcong. (U.S. Army photo, courtesy Shelby L. Stanton.)

tum of a determined enemy. Nor could they alter the troubled political landscape in South Vietnam. Johnson slated another 50,000 troops for war before the end of 1965, and the word was passed to General Westmoreland that more would be available if they were needed. America's role was no longer simply to provide aid and advice to the South Vietnamese. Now it was an American war, albeit a limited one.

Johnson, always wary of causing too much dissension at home or on the international front, did not commit America to the Vietnam conflict in one dramatic move. Instead troops trickled in slowly. It was an odd way to go to war, seldom, if ever, seen before in human history, and certainly never adopted by a country with the superpower status of the United States. The American troops in

An H-37 helicopter hovers over another copter as crewmen hook up a hoisting sling. Two soldiers (foreground) guard against a Vietcong attack. (U.S. Army photo.)

Vietnam in this early stage of the war represented a large enough force to put America's prestige in jeopardy, should they be pushed out, but too small a force to really take control of the war.

The Johnson administration had hoped that the measures taken would be enough not to destroy North Vietnam, but to kill Hanoi's will to carry on a war against South Vietnam. In the eyes of the administration, there was no need to mobilize the full support and resources of the United States—moral, political, and military—against the enemy. We would wait and see what his next move was, and respond accordingly.

The American government, then, had made a commitment to a war, but it was not like the commitment with which U.S. soldiers had gone off to fight in World War II. We would not devote all our force and energy to crushing the will of the North Vietnamese communists. Johnson would steer a middle course, hoping to preserve his domestic programs and expand civil rights, while at the same time staring down the communists in Asia.

But what was at stake for Americans in Southeast Asia, and what would winning there mean? What if the North Vietnamese just kept coming? This was a question that, for one reason or another, the administration had not fully considered. George Ball had warned that things could easily get out of hand if American forces were committed. The war could conceivably go on for years. Most men in the foreign policy establishment believed the United States could win a limited war. They minimized the tremendous difficulties which lay before them and their nation. Three more years of escalation were to follow.

4. Americans at War: 1966–1967

The great buildup of American troops in Vietnam in 1965 bought the tottering South Vietnamese government time to gather strength, and no doubt it discouraged the Vietcong, if only temporarily. Even before the first marines had waded ashore at Da Nang, however, the North Vietnamese had made a major strategic decision: They would attack central South Vietnam and attempt to cut the country in half. By late 1965, the NVA (North Vietnamese Army) had stored thousands of tons of supplies—ammunition, heavy guns, medical supplies—in Cambodia, near the border of South Vietnam.

The first major engagement of American and North Vietnamese soldiers was about to take place. It all began with an attack on the Special Forces camp at Plei Me situated east of the Ia Drang Valley, about thirty miles south of Pleiku. As soon as the disciplined NVA troops had laid siege to the camp, the U.S. First Air Cavalry Division was called in. U.S. helicopters were able to outmaneuver the NVA infantry, and the enemy force was cut to ribbons. The Americans now took the initiative, undertaking a search-and-destroy mission in the Ia Drang Valley.

Soon after landing, the 430 men of the Seventh Cavalry encountered stiff resistance from the NVA's Sixty-sixth Regiment, which heavily outnumbered them. One U.S. platoon was cut off from the other units, and had it not been for accurate supporting artillery fire on the night of November 14, the platoon might very well have been overrun.

The next day the Americans were reinforced by helicopter, but the NVA, determined to make a good showing in their first real combat with a large number of American troops, dug in and continued to fight hard. On November 17, after several days of furious combat, including hand-to-hand fighting, B-52s dropped their enormous payloads on the NVA positions. The fighting, however, persisted. American fighter-bombers were called into the fray soon after the American troops had regrouped. Their pilots dropped napalm on the NVA, engulfing one entire company in fire.

After the napalm sorties, the NVA's will to carry on the fight seemed to evaporate. They had seen firsthand how punishing American firepower could be, and the remainder of the North Vietnamese regular troops who had tangled with the U.S. Army fled into the jungle or back to the base camps in Cambodia. The battle of the Ia Drang Valley was over, and South Vietnam was still in one piece.

The success of the Ia Drang campaign gave heart to the men in Washington and Saigon. If the U.S. could inflict enough battlefield defeats on the North Vietnamese, eventually Hanoi's will was bound to crumble. Robert McNamara, the brillant business executive turned secretary of defense, loved statistics and data, and all the data, at this early stage in the war, seemed to suggest that we could solve the problem in Vietnam if we were willing to use the proper number of troops and the proper number of bombs. America's technological know-how and managerial expertise would ultimately result in such a high "body count" that Hanoi and the VC would be forced to cave in. Such was the theory of McNamara and the American strategists. And so the escalation of the war in Vietnam continued.

On December 31, 1965, there were 184,000 American troops in Vietnam. For all practical purposes, the Americans had taken over the war from the South Vietnamese. Between 1965 and 1967, South Vietnam was transformed into what seemed to some observers like one giant U.S. military installation. By the end of 1967, the secretary of defense presided over slightly less than half a million men there. Huge quantities of American goods flooded the country. Engineers built new harbors, airfields, supply depots, bridges, air-conditioned officers' clubs, and bowling alleys, all to service the vast numbers of Americans there to fight communism.

Just what kind of war did the American soldier encounter in Vietnam? It varied a great deal, as Colonel Summers points out in his foreword to this book. It was surely quite different from wars the American troops had been trained to fight. Like all foreign troops who had fought in Indochina, the Americans faced great difficulties in adjusting to the climate and to the unorthodox methods of a de-

A CH-54 "Flying Crane" lifts an 18,000-pound bridge span into place. American engineers in Vietnam possessed a dazzling ability to overcome natural obstacles. (U.S. Army photo.)

The face of jungle war. This U.S. marine is returning to his base after many days of combat. (U.S. Marine Corps photo.)

termined enemy. The monsoons and excessive heat for much of the year made moving in the bush an agonizing, wearying experience. The terrain of South Vietnam varies considerably. Many infantry soldiers, as they humped the trails through jungles, across rice paddies, and over mountains, came down with malaria or jungle rot, a condition affecting the skin which makes movement of any kind excruciatingly painful. Snakes, red ants, scorpions, leeches, and mud were their constant companions.

The American soldier frequently carried sixty pounds of equipment, sometimes even more, while on patrol. With all that weight, including a hot steel helmet, heat prostration was a real danger. Some soldiers died from it.

In pursuit of an elusive enemy, American troops often found themselves in combat at the time and place of the enemy's choosing. In the Mekong Delta, U.S. troops could be pinned down for hours at a time in the hot sun and flooded rice paddies. In the jungle areas, dense undergrowth had to be chopped down by hand, yard by yard. Firefights in the jungle often took place at very close quarters, a few dozen yards or less, and were extremely intense, with everyone firing on full automatic and lobbing grenades.

The American way of war in Vietnam required, as we have said, the employment of large amounts of firepower. By 1966, American ground forces had at their disposal an awesome array of weaponry and equipment to hunt down and destroy the enemy's armed forces. The helicopter, of course, has become the symbol of the war. The airmobile attacks mounted in the Ia Drang campaign became a favorite tactic of Army and Marine Corps field commanders. The advantages of having "heliborne" infantry were many. Soldiers could be lifted into small isolated LZs (landing zones) in a hurry, allowing American units to close in on an unsuspecting enemy.

Choppers made excellent aerial command posts, giving the officer in charge a previously impossible view of the entire battlefield, except where there was jungle canopy. Once troops had finished their mission, the helicopter could extract them quickly as well. Many a wounded soldier's life was saved by the heroic "medevac"

A U.S. Marine Corps tank shoots napalm at an enemy position. (U.S. Marine Corps photo.)

pilots who risked their own necks by landing on "hot" LZs to evacuate the wounded. If the treatment available at the base camps wasn't enough for the wounded soldiers, helicopters were used to ferry them to Army surgical hospitals, or in the case of the marines, to hospital ships stationed offshore. In Vietnam, 19 percent of those wounded died. In World War II, the figure was about 30 percent.

The helicopter, particularly the UH-1 Huey, was the workhorse of the battlefield. Air reconnaissance was another of its functions. The highly regarded military historian Shelby Stanton, himself a Special Forces veteran, provides an excellent description of how American ground forces and airpower teamed up to find and attack the NVA and VC in his *The Rise and Fall of an American Army:*

> On August 19, 1966, two light observation helicopters from Troop B [First Cavalry Division] spotted ten NVA soldiers hiding in the grass beside a trail. Two helicop-

ter gunships joined them four minutes later, and the troops' rifle platoon was sent aloft. The troop commander raced into his helicopter and was overhead in fifteen minutes. He marked a landing zone 150 feet away by dropping smoke, and the riflemen who arrived ten minutes later were set down. Meanwhile the two scout helicopters kept the NVA corralled. One made a low orbit, keeping them in constant sight, while the second flew a wider circle. The scout observer in the first craft discouraged two attempts at escape by firing short bursts from his M16 rifle.

The rifle platoon formed a diamond with its four squads and moved up to within 50 meters of the NVA, guided by the scout helicopter crew, who could see both groups. The platoon then swiftly fanned out into a line with one squad dropping back for rear security, and charged the pinned NVA soldiers. . . . Through the din of battle, the helicopters whisked overhead and radioed instructions. Two hours and twenty minutes from the first sighting the skirmish was ended. Sixteen NVA lay dead and nine wounded gave themselves up.[1]

The choppers performed an essential role in the clear-and-hold and search-and-destroy strategies developed by General William Westmoreland to meet the demands of a war without a single front. American and South Vietnamese troops were supposed to find, fix in place, fight, and destroy enemy forces, in that order. After the search-and-destroy operation was completed, local security forces, or sometimes elements of the ARVN, would be responsible for keeping the VC and NVA away from the local population.

Such an approach required great fighting prowess and aggressiveness, to be sure. But it also required an unusual degree of managerial skill. As the infantry troops patrolled the ground, their activities had to be coordinated with artillery support. The technologically sophisticated airplanes, helicopters, and communications devices used in the war required extensive maintenance. Coordination between base camps, the smaller fire-support bases, and airfields had to be precise. If it wasn't, it could mean that the enemy would escape, or that American lives would be needlessly lost.

To meet the extensive needs of the war effort, the vast majority of Americans in Vietnam were assigned to supply and support functions, not actual combat operations. There were twenty-seven major base camps built in the country, many of which resembled small cities. As time went on, a rift developed between those who fought and those who served in the relative comfort of the rear areas. It was an antagonism which festered, and ultimately hindered the prosecution of the war effort.

Much of the actual fighting during 1966 and 1967, especially the fighting involving American units responsible for a very specific area of operations, was initiated by the enemy, as we have noted. Because the VC, and to a lesser degree the NVA, knew the subtleties of the terrain, they avoided contact unless they felt they could escape from American heliborne troops and artillery if they had to.

When many people think of the Vietnam war, they imagine well-armed American troops charging after poorly equipped, pajama-clad guerrillas. There were many instances when this did happen, but by no means did combat in Vietnam always fit this stereotype. Small-unit clashes in Vietnam were vicious, bloody affairs, filled with terror and surprise, and the din of automatic-weapons and mortar fire. The histories of these engagements prepared by the individual units that fought them contain grisly accounts of soldiers fighting to the death not only with rifles and pistols, but with rocks, sticks, and bayonets.

The experience of patrolling in Vietnam in search of the enemy was a nerve-wracking one. Because this was a war without fronts, the soldier never knew when or where a firefight might occur. Enemy soldiers had a masterly grasp of camouflage techniques, and

Three Navy F-4B Phantom II jets in formation over South Vietnam. Jets from the Navy, the Air Force, and the Marines were indispensable weapons during America's war in Vietnam. They were used in support of ground troops and for strikes on important military targets. (U.S. Navy photo.)

many American patrols were ambushed. Even more unnerving than the unexpected fire from VC or NVA was the wide assortment of booby traps—pungi stakes dipped in poison and placed in carefully hidden pits, "bouncing Betty" mines designed to blow up at crotch level, and the like.

A favored NVA and VC tactic was the night frontal assault upon isolated American fire bases. In June 1966, for example, a company of marines defending a small airstrip at Dong Ha, five miles south of the DMZ (the Demilitarized Zone between North and South Vietnam), were attacked by a large force of NVA heading south. John Muir, a marine rifleman with the company, recounted what happened in Al Santoli's revealing collection of oral histories of the Vietnam War, *Everything We Had*:

> They [the NVA] put artillery up above us and were shooting down right on top of us. Rockets, machine-gun fire, rifle fire, everything you want. It was all point-blank.

> Helicopters kept resupplying us. They would take a quick low pass at the top of the hill and zoom by there, throwing out water and ammunition, grabbing as many wounded as they could. . . . We really didn't think about the future. I had no expectation of making it out of there . . . I had written us off. People were too tired to cry. . . . Sometimes they'd come on a dead run hollering and screaming. Usually they came in well-organized, well-controlled assault. We knew we were up against professionals; we knew we were up against some good ones.[2]

As it turned out, the marines took very heavy casualties at Dong Ha, but eventually, with the help of reinforcements, forced the NVA off the hill. In other battles Americans were not so lucky. It was not unheard-of for NVA or VC units to overrun entire American companies, particularly when bad weather prevented superior American air power from saving the day.

These years have been described as the time of the "big unit" war, and not without reason. The intensity and size of ground operations grew throughout the period as American troops tried to counteract the ever-increasing flow of NVA troops into the south. To get a clear idea of what these were like and what their purpose was, we will focus on two of the most important.

Operation Hastings was strictly a U.S. Marine affair. The marine effort in Vietnam was primarily restricted to I Corps, the northernmost military tactical zone in South Vietnam. When Hastings began in July 1966, it was the largest U.S. Marine operation in Vietnam to date. More important for our purposes, Hastings revealed much about the peculiarities of the Vietnam battlefield.

Like many U.S. operations, Hastings was triggered by enemy troop movement. During the first week in July, a recon squad had been dropped in behind enemy-controlled territory by helicopter. Once deployed, the squad found sure signs of large-scale NVA activity.

An aerial view of Camp Trai Bi, the first U.S. Army Special Forces camp established in War Zone C, northwest of Saigon, near the Cambodian border. Note the heavy flooding between the road at bottom and the chain of two-man foxholes on the perimeter of the base. (Courtesy Shelby L. Stanton.)

The 324B NVA Division was moving across the Ben Hai River into South Vietnam.

General Westmoreland believed that the wily General Giap was about to pounce upon the highly populated coast of Quang Tri Province, and he proceeded to order six marine infantry battalions, some 8,000 men, along with ARVN units to find the North Vietnamese troops and drive them back across the DMZ. On July 15, the first marines were airlifted into the Ngan River Valley, which is about five miles south of the border between North and South Vietnam. As two big CH-46 choppers made their descent to the LZ, they col-

Under fire at Mutters Ridge near the DMZ, marines hurl hand grenades and fire their weapons at enemy positions. (U.S. Marine Corps photo.)

lided and crashed, killing a number of marines. Still a third helicopter crashed attempting to put men on the ground. The NVA were firing on the choppers as they descended, and the battle had begun. Having made contact, the marines pushed toward the Ngan River in pursuit, but found themselves slowed down by the thick jungle, tall grass, and ferocious ground fire. Later that night, the NVA mounted a frontal assault on a battalion of marines it had managed to surround, but the tough infantrymen held their ground.

The next night it was more of the same. Heavy fighting in close quarters was general throughout the valley. Air strikes and artillery had to be called in dangerously close to the marine positions in order to fend off the NVA soldiers, more than a hundred of whom were killed on that night alone.

Throughout the course of Operation Hastings, marines would be drawn into firefights by the NVA's probes, many of which were cleverly designed to lure American troops out of their foxholes into ambushes. If the marines were able to fix the location of the enemy, most often the NVA soldiers would retreat into the darkness of the

The marine to the far right is firing an M-16, the standard American rifle after 1966. (U.S. Marine Corps photo.)

jungles, waiting for another chance to lure the Americans onto dangerous ground.

By August 3, Hastings officially ended, as contact with the enemy was sporadic. In fact, the marines had been successful in pushing the NVA back up north beyond the DMZ, but it was an uneasy success for the Americans, who had taken steep losses, by Vietnam War standards: 126 men killed, 448 wounded. Nor had the NVA forces been permanently destroyed. The marines were prohibited from crossing the DMZ in pursuit of the enemy by the rules of engagement set by Washington. The NVA would replenish their ranks and supplies and be back.

Another important and representative American military operation, Operation Cedar Falls, took place farther south, not far from Saigon itself, in January 1967. The "iron triangle" was the nickname for a Vietcong stronghold lying less than twenty miles northwest of South Vietnam's capital. It had been an area infested with VC since the French had lost their war in the 1950s. The American and South Vietnamese troops who had ventured into the area periodically hadn't the strength in numbers to eliminate the VC activity there. General Westmoreland hoped that Operation Cedar Falls would change this. Because the enemy was so firmly entrenched in the countryside, Westmoreland decided the entire area would have to be leveled.

Cedar Falls started off with B-52 sorties, which for several days hammered the sixty-square-mile plot of land. Then came airborne infantry. The American ground troops uncovered an astonishing array of underground complexes, complete with hospitals, offices, supply rooms, arsenals, sleeping quarters—a gigantic network which formed an integral part of the Vietcong military command for all of South Vietnam.

Some of the bravest American soldiers in Vietnam, called tunnel rats by their fellow soldiers, had to be sent down into the complexes to eliminate any remaining VC. They found very few, however.

An aerial view of the port of Quang Khe in North Vietnam, taken by a U.S. Air Force reconnaissance crew. Photographs like this one gave the American and South Vietnamese command a fairly accurate idea of NVA troop and supply movement. (U.S. Air Force photo.)

Most of the VC, knowing of the American operation, had fled into the jungle.

A primary objective of Cedar Falls was the elimination of the VC-fortified village of Ben Suc. Soldiers of the First Infantry Division, under the leadership of Lieutenant Colonel Alexander Haig (later secretary of state under Ronald Reagan), secured the village and removed the entire population—almost 6,000 people, along with their belongings and livestock—by air to a resettlement area.

Cedar Falls was neither a success nor a failure for the Americans. A trouble spot had been cleared of the enemy, at least for the time being. But ousting the VC couldn't have been done without destroying the entire village. The Vietnamese, people with exceptionally strong attachments to their ancestral lands, did not take kindly to the army that forcibly removed them from the triangle, even if the soldiers of that army explained that it was for their own good.

Back in the United States, television coverage of the razing of Ben Suc alarmed government policymakers and viewers alike. Were we saving the villages of Vietnam by destroying them? What good could possibly come about by forcible evacuation of Vietnamese farmers?

Reflecting on his lengthy service in Vietnam as an adviser to Vietnamese combat units, and later an infantry officer with the First Cavalry Division, William D. Neal got to the heart of the matter in an interview with the author. "We were able to really beat up the NVA and the VC when we could find their units," Neal said. "But we were losing the war for the villages. We just didn't have a workable doctrine for securing them and holding them away from the grasp of the Vietcong. The local troops, the regional and popular forces, just couldn't do the job, and we [the ARVN and Americans] couldn't hang around long enough to hold a village."

The remainder of 1967 saw countless military engagements between Americans and the communists, most of which, by the grisly standard of the body count, the Americans won. In fact, the Americans won all the major battles. And yet as the year dragged on,

The villagers of Ben Suc gather in the town center for evacuation by helicopter. (Wide World Photos.)

neither the American people nor their president took heart from the victories. The reason for this was quite simple. The battlefield victories didn't seem to be moving the war in the right direction. Ho Chi Minh seemed undaunted by the high toll North Vietnam was paying by defying the American military. Pessimistic reports seemed to appear almost daily on President Johnson's desk, claiming that the bombing and the war of attrition waged against North Vietnam and the VC had failed to dent the will of Hanoi to carry on the fight.

Almost since the first U.S. Marines had landed in March 1965, attempts had been made to negotiate a settlement between the two nations, but nothing at all was to come of these efforts. Neither side was willing to compromise on its basic objectives enough to get the other side to the bargaining table. Several conferences and secret talks were canceled at the last minute out of lack of trust, despite the efforts of intermediaries from a number of nations, including Canada, Poland, and the Soviet Union.

Inability to get to the negotiating table was hardly the only problem. By the end of 1967, with public confidence in the Johnson administration on the wane, a number of senior advisers and civilians working in the Defense Department were questioning whether the United States could ever win its war in Vietnam, let alone win it quickly. Secretary of Defense McNamara, long a spokesman for the administration on Vietnam and perhaps the key architect of America's war, was rapidly losing enthusiasm. More than anyone else, he had believed that the United States could, through superior technology and firepower, force the communists to withdraw, but his recent trips to Vietnam had disillusioned him. Privately, he advocated that the United States abandon the search-and-destroy strategy and halt the bombing of North Vietnam, which, according to CIA studies, had minimal effects upon the ability of the north to fight the war in the south. Search-and-destroy operations had cut up General Giap's armed forces, to be sure, but they had not created stability or security in South Vietnam's 16,000 villages.

General William C. Westmoreland and Lieutenant General Creighton W. Abrams inspect the troops during a parade. Abrams took over command of American troops in Vietnam from Westmoreland. (U.S. Marine Corps photo.)

On the other hand, members of the military leadership, especially General Westmoreland and Admiral Sharp, pleaded with the president to call up the armed forces reserves so more soldiers—there now being half a million already in the country—could be brought in to finish the job. Dean Rusk and the man who had replaced National Security Adviser McGeorge Bundy, Walt Rostow, supported their claims.

For his part, President Johnson could not bear the thought of America's allowing South Vietnam to slip away at the negotiating table. He simply would not be the first president to lose a war. But nor could he face the idea of increased taxes to finance a war. If Vietnam continued to drain the coffers of the government, Johnson's dream of the Great Society would vanish into thin air. And so he hesitated, making no firm decision at all. Meanwhile, the tension between the warring factions ate away slowly at the administration, poisoning the atmosphere and hampering clear thinking precisely when it was most needed.

By the end of 1967, Johnson was a frustrated, embittered man, trapped by a war with no end and no escape route. As time went on and the dismal reports of a long war flowed into the White House, LBJ became increasingly distrustful of those who disagreed with his Vietnam policies, even if those people were his handpicked advisers. A sense of despair seemed to permeate the White House. Johnson, wrote David Halberstam in his brilliant book *The Best and the Brightest,*

> would talk with some fatalism about the trap he had built for himself, with an almost plaintive cry for some sort of help. But these moments were rare indeed, very private, and more often than not they would soon be replaced by wild rages against any critic who might voice the most gentle doubt of the [Vietnam] policy and the direction in which it was taking the country.
>
> So instead of leading, he was immobilized, surrounded, seeing critics everywhere.[3]

If things were dismal in Washington, they were far worse among the populace of South Vietnam. Many problems were unwittingly fueled by the American presence and prosecution of the war. Approximately 25 percent of the rural population of South Vietnam became refugees of war. As American planes and artillery tore up the countryside, poor farmers fled toward Saigon, Hue, Da Nang, and other cities, settling on the outskirts of town in shacks made from American refuse. Amid abject poverty, prostitution and disease flourished.

Aid funds and supplies intended to ease the burden of the refugees were frequently stolen by corrupt importers, making an already frail economy even worse. Slowly but surely, South Vietnam became more and more dependent upon America to keep it afloat, adding legitimacy to the communist claim that the South Vietnamese were puppets of the United States. The Thieu-Ky regime tottered along, barely managing to maintain its position amid the crises engendered by the war and internal tensions between the Buddhists and the government.

The South Vietnamese armed forces seemed content to rely upon the Americans to do much of the fighting. The notorious corruption problems and political promotion of officers continued to hamper the ARVN's ability to carry the fight to the enemy.

The cultural barriers between the American and ARVN troops were, of course, substantial, and they contributed to the woes. Americans knew little about Vietnamese life and traditions, and many of the South Vietnamese soldiers resented their well-off foreign allies. Captain William Neal told the author that when he was serv-

Innocent victims of war, these children await medical attention. Hundreds of thousands of Vietnamese children were maimed, orphaned, or left homeless by the war. (U.S. Army photo.)

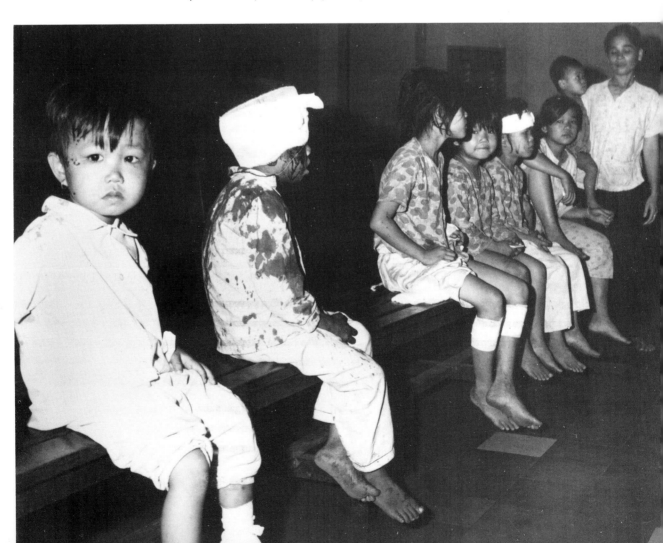

ing as an adviser to the ARVN in 1967, 5 to 10 percent of the ARVN soldiers in his unit were suspected of being sympathetic to the Vietcong cause. Some of the experienced officers in the ARVN had been trained by the French and had little in common with the soldiers they commanded. Security leaks were for these reasons a nagging problem. Captain Neal brought this home in a brief anecdote: After a VC attack which had threatened to overrun Neal's fire base had been turned back, a dead Vietcong soldier had been found with a detailed map of the entire fire base, gun positions and all. Neal saw his own name marked on the map next to his sleeping quarters.

In the fall of 1967, as American planes continued to bomb the Ho Chi Minh Trail and American troops prowled across South Vietnam in pursuit of the elusive enemy, support at home for the war effort lagged. Each night on the news, the gruesome body-count figures—of American, South Vietnamese, and communist soldiers—grew, but there was little evidence that the will of the North Vietnamese or VC was flagging.

In November 1967, President Johnson responded to the deteriorating public confidence by calling his field commander back home. Perhaps the square-jawed, resolute General Westmoreland would be able to rally support for the cause. As usual, Westmoreland's public statements about the war were optimistic. The bloody fighting at Dak To, he said, was about to be won by the Americans. That battle was the beginning of a major defeat for the enemy. Indeed, the battle was a great success *by conventional standards*. The U.S. Army devoured the NVA, killing more than 1,400. But high body counts, it was becoming increasingly apparent, were not going to be enough to win the war in Vietnam.

In private, Westmoreland said that if the president kept the ceiling on American troops in Vietnam at 470,000, "in the end we would do little better than hold our own."[4] Even if the United States escalated the war by introducing an additional 200,000 troops, the conflict would drag on for another two years. Johnson was caught in a trap. He dreaded the thought of escalation, of calling up America's reserve forces and raising taxes, with all the social backlash that would entail. But he dreaded the idea of an interminable conflict sapping young Americans' lives even more. And he grew weary of conflict with the press, which no longer supported "his" war.

And so he made one of many inexplicable decisions: He would grant Westmoreland more troops, but not enough to do the job. The new ceiling would be 525,000 men—enough to stave off defeat, but not enough to win. And he would stage an all-out effort to reverse the tide of negative opinion about Vietnam in the United States. Government "truth teams" were sent out to spread the word that

An ARVN patrol meets with the elders of a Cham village in South Vietnam. American adviser William D. Neal is at far right. The Cham are one of the many ethnic minorities in Vietnam. (Courtesy William D. Neal.)

The leaders of South Vietnam during the period of U.S. escalation: Nguyen Van Thieu (front, left) and Nguyen Cao Ky (front, right), shown here before a parade honoring the South Vietnamese armed forces. (Courtesy Shelby L. Stanton.)

the United States was going to hold the line and win in Vietnam. They were armed, as usual, with a wealth of statistics and reports hailing progress on the ground war against the NVA and VC, the air war, and the pacification of the villages.

In December 1967, the president expanded the number of targets that American planes could attack. On the ground, there were reports that American and ARVN forces were chasing the NVA into its sanctuaries in Cambodia. The Cambodian head of state, Prince Sihanouk, filed formal protest, as did the Laotians, who were also fearful that the Vietnam War would spread deeper into their territory. The forays into Vietnam's neighbors foreshadowed far greater horrors for the Cambodians and Laotians.

As another year of war drew to a close, General Westmoreland told a worried Congress, "We have reached an important point where the end begins to come into view."[5] Those who believed the statement accurate were in for a terrible surprise. The surprise was called Tet.

5. Tet 1968 and Afterward: The Turning of the Tide

Saigon, the sprawling, bustling capital of South Vietnam, was in many ways the heart of the American and South Vietnamese war effort against the North Vietnamese and the Vietcong. This pleasant, largely French-built city had become swollen with the refugees of war and with servicemen on leave from the combat zones and by 1968 had a population of two million. Since most of the highest-ranking officers and government officials were in Saigon, so was the press corps. Hundreds of correspondents from around the world were crammed into Saigon's hotels. Surprisingly, since the Americans had been in Vietnam, Saigon had been relatively free of violence. But on the morning of January 31, 1968, the great Tet holiday marking the beginning of the lunar new year (similar to New Year's Eve or Christmas), the Vietnam war came to Saigon. And it came in full force.

At about 1:30 A.M. the guards at the presidential palace in the center of the city heard sounds coming from outside the gate. Suddenly a B-40 rocket ripped through the wall, and fourteen soldiers of the highly trained Vietcong C-10 Battalion rushed through the hole, firing automatic weapons. The security forces inside returned fire, driving the VC back out of the palace and across the street into an unfinished apartment house. There the VC dug in and prepared for the inevitable counterassault.

An hour or so after the attack on the presidential palace another team from the C-10 Battalion attacked the seemingly unattackable—the U.S. embassy, situated just a few blocks from the palace. The South Vietnamese police who were patrolling just out-

A view of the hole in the American embassy wall through which the Vietcong gained entrance to the compound. (U.S. Army photo.)

side the wall fled as soon as the Vietcong unit began firing. The sappers, after blasting through the eight-foot-high wall surrounding the compound, killed two of the three marine guards that were on duty that night. It took the Americans and the South Vietnamese forces six hours to regain control. It would take two days—and the firepower of a couple of tanks—to subdue the members of the C-10 Battalion in the apartment house across from the presidential palace.

These sapper attacks on the highly visible symbols of the allied governments were at once fierce, daring, and foolhardy. But they were in fact only two of more than a hundred carefully coordinated attacks carried out by both the Vietcong and the NVA against major

A Vietcong corpse lies on the embassy grounds shortly after the attack. (U.S. Army photo.)

U.S. soldiers take cover behind the wall of Bachelor Officers Quarters #3, which was assaulted by the VC during Tet. (U.S. Army photo.)

military installations and cities in the south. Within twenty-four hours, the communists had rocketed the great American base at Cam Ranh Bay. They assaulted General Westmoreland's headquarters fifteen miles north of Saigon, at Long Binh, with both mortars and rockets. The U.S. 199th Infantry Brigade countered the Vietcong attack with the aide of withering helicopter gunship fire.

To the south, in the populous, fertile Mekong Delta region, thirteen of sixteen provincial capitals were attacked simultaneously. Although the American and ARVN troops were quick to respond to the invasion of the cities and bases—in many cases taking back territory from the VC and NVA with superior firepower and great courage—the ferocity and sheer number of assaults stunned the allied forces. They simply could not believe that the enemy was capable of planning and carrying out an offensive of such magnitude.

As they learned of the ferocity and extent of the communist attacks, American troops everywhere in Vietnam were shocked. Just two months earlier, Westmoreland had assured the troops—and

President Johnson in Washington—that the end had come into view. Communist troop strength should have been sapped by American and South Vietnamese firepower to a point where such an offensive would have been impossible to undertake.

President Thieu had allowed many of the South Vietnamese soldiers responsible for guarding the population centers to go home to their villages for the Tet holiday. General Westmoreland had wrongly believed that the communists were more interested in capturing territory near the American combat base at Khe Sanh, set in the lush, green hills of I Corps, near the DMZ.

General Fred Weyand, who was in central Vietnam at the time of the attacks, described the maps in his operations center as lighting up "like pinball machines."[1] One city and then another came under attack.

In America, the nightly news showed images of men in desperate battle—wounded soldiers being taken out of combat zones by helicopter with fighting still going on, corpses littering the U.S. embassy grounds and the streets of South Vietnam's largest cities. American field commanders were reporting record casualties throughout the country. It was hard to escape the conclusion, in the weeks following the first attacks, that the optimism of the high command had lulled Americans and South Vietnamese alike into a false sense of security. Once again, the enemy had been underestimated.

How could the communists have done it, and what did they hope to achieve? The decision to launch the attack had been made in Hanoi in July 1967. General Giap, of course, was personally charged with preparing strategy.

In August, the North Vietnamese began to send increasingly large quantities of military equipment to the Vietcong units in the south. Communist political cadres in South Vietnam began the work that, according to revolutionary strategy, must go hand in hand with military operations against the Americans and South Vietnamese. They distributed leaflets and made radio broadcasts to the South Viet-

An American billet after a VC attack during Tet. (U.S. Army photo.)

namese people, urging them to abandon their "puppet" government, supported by the American "aggressors."

Several months before the major offensive, Giap launched a series of attacks on the five northern provinces in an attempt to pull allied forces away from the cities. In unofficial talks with U.S. officials, the National Liberation Front—the political arm of the Vietcong—began to take a more flexible approach in dealing with the Americans, hoping to arouse suspicions within the South Vietnamese government that the United States was negotiating behind its back.

The main objective of the offensive was to spark uprisings among the people of South Vietnam against the United States and the government in Saigon. If the attacks failed to accomplish this, Giap hoped that the confusion they caused would force the Americans to put pressure on the South Vietnamese government to improve its performance, thereby increasing the tension between the two major allies. And, of course, Giap realized that if American casualties were high, the will of the American people to make the sacrifices of war—already weakening—would be weakened further.

It became apparent within a couple of days that the attacks on South Vietnam were not going to spark the uprising the NVA leadership had hoped for. Within a week, communist forces had been pushed out of every major stronghold in the three southern military regions. But up in I Corps, it was a different story. There the NVA had captured Hue, one of Vietnam's oldest, most prized cities. To the northwest of Hue, in Khe Sanh, 6,000 U.S. Marines were surrounded by as many as 20,000 crack North Vietnamese troops. They had been shelled heavily with mortars and heavy artillery since January 21, more than a week before Tet. Events in both Hue and Khe Sanh would have a profound impact not only on the outcome of the Tet offensive, but on the entire direction of the Vietnam War.

Hue, the third-largest city in Vietnam, had been the capital of the country before its partition in 1954. Until the Tet offensive, it had been spared the destruction and carnage that by 1968 had afflicted so much of the Vietnamese countryside. There was a large university there, built by the French, and a prestigious preparatory school, called the Quoc Hoc High School, where many of the leaders of the country, including Ngo Dinh Diem, General Giap, and Ho Chi Minh, had been educated. At the center of the city lay the Imperial Citadel, a huge stone fortress built at the beginning of the nineteenth century. High, thick walls formed the border of the fortress on all sides except the southeast, where the Song Huong, or Perfume River, ran its course. It was within the confines of the Imperial Citadel that the communist troops would do battle with American and South Vietnamese forces for three long weeks before being subdued.

The attack began, like so many attacks of the offensive, in the early morning of January 31. Two NVA battalions charged through the western gates of the city, north of the river, while other communist units assaulted the MACV (Military Assistance Command, Vietnam) compound to the south. Despite some early warnings of increased communist military activity in the area, both the South Vietnamese, responsible for the defense of the city, and the American marines stationed at a nearby base were caught off guard. Within hours almost the entire city—hospitals, schools, and residential areas—was under communist control.

The first company of marines called in to relieve the besieged troops of the ARVN First Division, whose headquarters were inside the citadel itself, were stopped cold in their attempt to cross the Perfume River by rockets, heavy automatic-weapons fire, and mortars. The NVA and Vietcong attacks had been carefully planned, and their troops would not be easily displaced, given the very favorable defensive positions they were able to take up within the citadel's walls.

The fighting that ensued over the next few weeks was not at all like the fighting we think of as being typical of the Vietnam War. It didn't take place in the rice fields or in the lush mountainous regions, where actually seeing the enemy was a rarity. Instead, it occurred within the confines of city streets and alleys. And it was ferocious. It took the U.S. Marines, so well known for their tenacity and fighting spirit, four days to clear the four blocks of territory from the MACV compound to the hospital situated near the southern bank of the river.

The well-trained, highly motivated communists had to be removed from the entrenched positions the hard way—marine rifle squads flushed them out, house by house. Casualties among the marines and the South Vietnamese units were extremely heavy.

Across the river, additional U.S. forces were called in to help take the citadel, and the Imperial Palace located within its walls, in which the communists had set up their command post. Slowly but surely, the allied troops pushed the resistance into the southern sector of the citadel, but not until they were forced to call in air strikes from U.S. A-4 jets and naval gunfire on the enemy positions.

The soldiers and marines responsible for dislodging the enemy fought under the worst possible conditions. The weather was un-

A U.S. marine takes cover by a garden wall in the city of Hue. (U.S. Army photo, courtesy Shelby L. Stanton.)

usually stormy and cold for this time of year in Vietnam. The troops got little or no sleep and few reinforcements, and what little progress they made cost them dearly in blood. Michael Herr, a correspondent who covered the battle for Hue, captured the atmosphere perfectly in his classic book *Dispatches*:

> Going in, there were sixty of us packed into a deuce-and-a-half, one of eight trucks moving in convoy from Phu Bai, bringing in over 300 replacements for the casualties taken in the earliest fighting south of the Perfume River. There had been a harsh, dark storm going on for days, and it turned the convoy route into a mudbed. It was terribly cold in the trucks, and the road was covered with leaves that had either been blown off the trees by the storm or torn away by our artillery. . . . Many of the houses had completely collapsed, and not one had been left without pitting from shell fragments. Hundreds of refugees held to the side of the road as we passed, many of them wounded. The kids would laugh and shout, the old would look on with that silent tolerance for misery that made so many Americans uneasy, which was usually misread as indifference. . . . The houses that we passed so slowly made good cover for snipers, and one B-40 rocket could have made casualties out of a whole truckload of us. All the grunts were whistling, and no two were whistling the same tune, it sounded like a locker room before a game nobody wanted to play.[2]

Finally, on the morning of February 24, South Vietnamese units actually got into the Imperial Palace itself. Before the assault, they had anticipated heavy resistance; they met with none. The only NVA they found were dead. The others had vanished from the city overnight, fleeing westward to sanctuaries in Laos.

Marines patrol the battle-scarred streets of Hue in February 1968. (U.S. Marine Corps photo.)

The story of the battle for Hue is a significant part of the story of the Vietnam War. It was the most vicious and costly battle of the offensive for both sides, and it revealed something about the character and methods of the enemy. After the battle, when civilians of the city were interviewed, it was revealed that the communists had actually set up a "revolutionary" government soon after taking control. When they entered the city, they had with them a list of "cruel tyrants and reactionaries"—people who were associated with the Americans, or the South Vietnamese government, or both. The evidence shows that these people were systematically collected, mercilessly killed without any pretense of a trial, and buried in shallow graves. According to one source, 200 Roman Catholic males were rounded up for what the communists said was political reeducation. None of the men were ever heard from again.

Estimates of the total number of assassinations range from 500 to 5,000. Those executed were hardly the only civilians to suffer at Hue. Many more were killed in the small-arms crossfire that raged for weeks, and by the naval gunfire the Americans used to dislodge the NVA and Vietcong. More than 200 U.S. Marines and other U.S. troops lost their lives in the fighting; 1,200 were wounded. But the communist forces had paid a heavy price. They lost as many as 8,000 men.

Hue marked the longest battle of the Tet offensive. But when the last communist troops had been driven from the old capital, the allied forces couldn't afford to rest easy. Up in Quang Tri Province, eighteen miles from the DMZ, 6,000 marines were under siege at Khe Sanh, the combat base that rested on one of the many hills in the area. Estimates of the number of enemy troops varied, but everyone knew that a number of crack NVA divisions had been spotted near the base.

The main road leading to Khe Sanh, Route 9, was controlled by the enemy, so the marines' supplies had to be brought in by air. Being close to the DMZ, Khe Sanh was isolated from allied military outposts; and yet, in the late winter and early spring of 1968, holding the line at Khe Sanh became an American obsession. Everyone wondered if the outnumbered forces there could withstand an all-out NVA assault—an assault which seemed more and more likely after the outbreak of the Tet offensive.

There were a number of reasons why Khe Sanh was the object of such intense scrutiny. General Westmoreland saw the base as a key blocking point should the NVA try to invade the northern provinces with infantry and tanks. And even if the NVA didn't actually launch an invasion, Khe Sanh would serve as a kind of magnet, drawing large numbers of NVA units to within range of American firepower. In other words, Khe Sanh might easily evolve into the kind of battle the U.S. armed forces were best at fighting—a conventional knock-down-drag-out fight between large numbers of troops supported by heavy artillery and air power. If the NVA would come out and fight, some American strategists reasoned, the overwhelming firepower of the American and South Vietnamese forces would, once and for all, crush the will of the enemy to carry on.

And so when intelligence reports in the winter of 1967 showed increased NVA activity in the area, Westmoreland ordered the marines to reinforce the base and prepare for battle.

The Marine Corps leadership was somewhat skeptical. Was the base really worth it? Was it possible to hold, given that it was so far north in the rugged highlands, so close to the DMZ? But Westmoreland's belief that something big was brewing near the DMZ was supported by increased activity on the Ho Chi Minh Trail, and by a bizarre incident which occurred near the perimeter of the base itself on January 2, 1968. On that day, marine guards shot five NVA soldiers wearing marine uniforms. They turned out to be not regular scouts, but NVA officers. Why would they have been so close to the base? What would the NVA's next move be?

The marines began to dig in, both on the base itself and on the six surrounding hills. They built mortarproof bunkers, put up German razor wire, and dug trenches for protection against the big Soviet and Chinese artillery that the NVA had within range of the base.

A fire base atop Hill 861, to the west of the main base at Khe Sanh. (U.S. Marine Corps photo.)

On the night of January 20, elite NVA units attacked Hill 861, to the west of the base. Although the marines on the hill eventually repulsed the attack, the NVA inflicted heavy casualties. It was easy to read this action as a test assault, preparation for a major attack on the combat base itself.

The following day, January 21, the communists began to shell the combat base. A rocket landed inside the main ammunition dump, exploding some 1,500 tons—90 percent of the marines' ammo—and starting a fire that would rage for more than twenty-four hours. Supplying the base by air was far from an easy task, because the runway was damaged by the continual shelling. Things got so bad that the Air Force stopped trying to fly in its biggest transport plane; it proved to be too easy a target for the NVA gunners.

The tension mounted after the NVA overran the neighboring Special Forces camp at Lang Vei on February 2. For the first time in the war, the NVA had used tanks. Would those same tanks—Soviet in origin—be used in an attack on Khe Sanh by the 20,000 or so NVA regulars estimated to be in the area?

For a time in the early months of 1968, after the Vietcong and NVA advances in the cities of South Vietnam had been checked, holding Khe Sanh was a primary concern not just of military men fighting in the war, but of President Johnson himself. In fact, Johnson had a model of the base constructed in the basement of the White House. In an unprecedented move, he asked every one of the Joint Chiefs of Staff—the highest officers in each branch of the American armed forces—to sign a document claiming that the base could *and would* be held. Many Americans, both in Vietnam and at home, feared that Khe Sanh could become the American Dien Bien Phu. Dien Bien Phu, you remember, was the scene of the final defeat of the French in the First Indochina War.

To ensure that there would be no such defeat at Khe Sanh, General Westmoreland planned to saturate the areas of NVA activity near the base with bombs. The plan, called Operation Niagara, involved some 2,000 aircraft. The idea was to inflict such heavy casualties by aerial bombardment that the NVA simply wouldn't be able to attack the base. On an average day during the Khe Sanh siege, American planes flew 300 sorties against NVA positions. B-52s—the largest American bombers—dropped their massive payloads on NVA positions every ninety minutes.

Despite this overwhelming air strength, the NVA continued to shell the marines. This constant shelling and the knowledge that the NVA were digging tunnels closer and closer to the perimeter kept the Americans on a constant state of alert, night and day. Here is Michael Herr's description of a night at Khe Sanh:

> Flares were dropping everywhere around the fringes of the perimeter, laying a dead white light on the high ground rising from the piedmont. There would be doz-

Survivors of a thirty-man patrol outside the perimeter of Khe Sanh struggle to return to safety with their wounded. The marines were ambushed by the NVA. (Robert Ellison/Black Star.)

Marines duck for cover as an NVA artillery shell explodes at Khe Sanh. (Robert Ellison/Black Star.)

ens of them at once sometimes, trailing an intense smoke, dropping white-hot sparks, and it seemed as though anything caught in their range would be made still, like figures in a game of living statues. There would be the muted rush of illumination rounds, fired from 60mm mortars inside the wire, dropping magnesium—brilliant above the NVA trenches for a few seconds, outlining the gaunt, flat spread of mahogany trees, giving the landscape a ghastly clarity, and dying out. . . .[3]

As the battle of Khe Sanh continued, the marines would send out patrols up to 500 meters beyond the base perimeter. By late March, the patrols were getting into fewer and fewer firefights. Signs of enemy activity were found less frequently. Intelligence reports at the time seemed to confirm the eerie truth: The NVA had abandoned their tunnels and their trails; they had left behind only the dead.

The First Cavalry Airmobile Division was called in to relieve the marines, who had been living in half-blown-up, rat-infested bunkers for more than two months. They cleared out what little resistance they met on Route 9 and around the base itself. The siege at Khe Sanh was over.

But what had it all meant? Why had the NVA remained for so long, with so many troops, against such overwhelming air power, only to abandon the area? Was it simply a costly diversionary effort to get Westmoreland to send troops up north, away from the cities, to increase the chances for the Tet attacks to succeed? The experts disagree to this day. Khe Sanh, one of the most famous battles of the Vietnam War, remains, like the war itself, something of a mystery.

When the battles of the massive Tet offensive were over, there was little doubt that the major objectives of the Vietcong and the North Vietnamese hadn't been realized. The people of South Vietnam had not risen up against their government. And wherever the attacks on the South Vietnamese cities occurred, American and ARVN troops ultimately repulsed the attackers.

An early written assessment of the offensive by the National Liberation Front (NLF) went so far as to blame the armed forces for failing to create the right conditions for the masses to turn against their "oppressors." And, of course, the communists, particularly the Vietcong, suffered tremendous losses. Some experts believe that the Vietcong were virtually destroyed after Tet, having lost approximately 60 percent of their men, including many political cadres that had been given rifles.

And yet, if the communists had not won in a military sense, they had seriously damaged the pacification program—the American effort to bolster popular support for the government of South Vietnam by providing security and increasing economic prosperity in the villages.

As the full extent of the offensive became known in the early spring of 1968, and General Westmoreland requested that an additional 200,000 troops be sent to Vietnam, it became increasingly apparent that those reports sent to Washington before Tet, which detailed large enemy body counts, progress in reforming the South Vietnamese government, and erosion of the enemy's will to fight, had been poor barometers of success.

The American people, having sent their young men to war in Southeast Asia in increasing numbers for three years, felt they had been duped. Too many men had died. Americans were willing to fight in Vietnam, but only for a defensible cause, only if they could be shown that progress was being made. By mid-March, popular approval for the president's handling of the war had fallen from 40 to 26 percent. As historian Stanley Karnow put it in *Vietnam: A History*, "The country's trust in his [the president's] authority had evaporated. His credibility—the key to a president's capacity to govern—was gone."[4]

Soon after the offensive, President Johnson assembled a task force to examine future U.S. policy in Vietnam. The recommendation of the group, which included many highly respected foreign-policy experts, was that the United States could not win the war at any time soon, and that it should begin to decrease the American military presence in Vietnam.

The recommendations of this group, along with growing popular and congressional pressure, led to a dramatic speech by the president on March 31, 1968. Lyndon Johnson announced a halt to all bombing of North Vietnam, except for the area just north of the DMZ. His hope was that such an act would bring the north to the bargaining table. Johnson wanted to talk peace.

At the end of the speech, the president, visibly exhausted by the strains of leading the nation in an unpopular war, announced that he would not seek the presidency again. Three days later, to the surprise of most observers, the North Vietnamese agreed to open negotiations with the United States.

After weeks of haggling over the site, it was agreed to meet in Paris at the Majestic Hotel. The venerable Averell Harriman, one of America's most distinguished diplomats, would head the American delegation. Xuan Thuy, the secretary of the central committee of the North Vietnamese Communist Party, would head the North Vietnamese party. Talks began on May 13.

Talking, however, didn't mean an end to the fighting. Both sides were anxious to bargain from a position of strength, and as they prepared for the battle at the conference table in Paris, the soldiers kept up the battle for control over South Vietnamese territory. In April, a combined force of American and ARVN troops, some 50,000 men, engaged the enemy in a large-scale counteroffensive. With the help of forest fires, this force drove the communists out of the U Minh forest in the Mekong Delta.

In Operation Delaware, U.S. troops journeyed into the forbidding A Shau Valley in I Corps, which contained a base camp for more than 5,000 North Vietnamese troops. Thousands of pounds of B-52 bombs weren't enough to silence NVA guns, and on the very first day of the operation, ten helicopters were lost. The NVA opted to evade U.S. forces on the ground, leaving behind huge quantities of ammunition and weapons which might have been intended for yet another offensive.

In May, the communists once again attacked Saigon. The attacks came in two waves, and the fighting was bloody and intense. Civilian casualties were exceptionally high, because the ARVN and the U.S. forces continued to root out the North Vietnamese and VC with napalm and other highly explosive materials, leaving thousands of Saigon residents homeless and resentful.

The purpose of the attack on Saigon had been to keep the pres-

May 1968: Vietcong bodies lie in the street in Cholon, the Chinese district near Saigon. ARVN Rangers mill about behind the corpses. (Courtesy Shelby L. Stanton.)

sure on the South Vietnamese government, to challenge its ability to meet the needs of its refugee-ridden population. There was little question that the South Vietnamese government had its hands full. The Tet offensive had left 14,000 civilians dead, and many government services were out of action for months after the attacks. Under constant pressure from the Americans, President Thieu had attempted to pull the various factions—Buddhists, Catholics, and various other religious sects which had some political power—together to confront the destruction. Most observers, though, felt that Thieu had only marginal success in doing so. Having spoken to Vietnamese on the scene immediately after Tet, the journalist Robert Shaplen reported that "they sound more and more like men who are suffering from an incurable malady."[5]

Political rivalry seemed to grow more rather than less vicious in the face of adversity. Vice President Ky conspired to challenge

A soldier fires his M-60 machine gun at an enemy position in the second attack on Saigon in May 1968. (U.S. Army photo.)

Thieu, only to be thwarted by the American embassy's outspoken support for the president, and by some shrewd, timely dismissals of Ky supporters in top posts. More important, Thieu, like many Vietnamese, felt increasingly anxious and bitter about the United States. Thieu feared a sellout at the Paris talks, which he had refused to participate in. There were even rumors that the American delegation might accept a coalition government including Vietcong representatives, something which the South Vietnamese government dreaded, and that the Americans had known in advance of the Tet offensive and had waited to see if the South Vietnamese really wanted to fight for their country before intervening.

In July, Thieu met with President Johnson in Honolulu and obtained a promise from the American that no coalition government would be agreed to in Paris. The Saigon government would participate in drawing up any final settlement, according to the statement issued at the end of the conference. Nonetheless, fear of abandonment continued in South Vietnam, and not without reason. America was in the process of changing course in Vietnam, and the winds of change suggested that the Americans were no longer seeking an outright victory, but merely intended to nurse Saigon along and get their own troops out of Southeast Asia.

Throughout the fall and early winter of 1968, it was more of the same in Vietnam: deadlock at the conference table, while the Americans refused to halt their heavy bombing and the North Vietnamese continued to push their troops and supplies down the Ho Chi Minh Trail in record-breaking numbers. Peace was a long way off. As the South Vietnamese attempted to repair the damage done to the pacification program, the NVA and VC pressed on doggedly, menacing the cities with rocket attacks and taking advantage of the decreased number of troops in the countryside. Hanoi hoped that the Americans' will to continue what was by now the longest war in American history would diminish with each new American casualty.

Beginning in January 1969, the communists would face a new adversary. For that was when Richard Nixon became the thirty-seventh president of the United States and the commander in chief of U.S. forces in Vietnam. Before we turn to the war under Nixon, we are going to explore two facets of the long war in Vietnam in detail—dissent over U.S. policy at home, and the nature of America's enemy in Vietnam.

6. Dissent and Protest: The Vietnam War in America

By the time of the Tet offensive, four American presidential administrations had grappled with the ever-changing military and political perplexities of Vietnam. Southeast Asia had figured prominently in American foreign policy for more than fifteen years, but solutions to the myriad problems in Vietnam still seemed depressingly remote. More ominously, those who ran the war were more divided than ever before on what was to be done in Vietnam. The bureaucracies continued to quarrel; the military men pressed to enlarge the war, while a group of civilian planners were saying that no amount of military force would solve the problems of South Vietnam.

Disagreement—passionate disagreement—about what the U.S. role in Vietnam ought to be was nothing new. Right from the start of the American effort to save South Vietnam from communism, there had been those who believed it would prove to be a very costly mistake, sure to result in many lost lives for a dubious cause. Others felt that it might even prove impossible to save South Vietnam at all, given the extent of U.S. commitments in other parts of the world.

Some of the most prominent early dissenters were military men. Among them was General Matthew Ridgway, the highly respected American commander of United Nations forces in Korea. The general had warned that the United States could well suffer disaster if it became committed to defending a fledgling state in Asia. It wasn't only the possibility of Chinese intervention that prompted such counsel. Ridgway believed there would be too many logistical difficulties in trying to supply ground forces so far from the American

Two American soldiers along with the body of a fallen comrade await an evacuation helicopter in a jungle clearing. (AP/Wide World Photos.)

mainland. Nor were American troops trained for the kind of warfare they were likely to encounter in Vietnam.

As the picture of our South Vietnamese allies became more precise, there were other skeptics, both inside the government and out, who said that the leaders of South Vietnam were simply too incompetent, too anxious to take advantage of the immense resources of the United States, to bear down on the communists who threatened to take over their country. Could these people be counted on to win the allegiance of the people?

By the time the Kennedy administration was formulating its Vietnam policy, insightful men like George Ball, the under secretary of state, were arguing that despite reports of progress filed from the various agencies and military advisers, the war would be far more costly and painful for Americans than most people thought. When in the early 1960s Ball estimated that the war might someday require as many as 300,000 U.S. troops, President Kennedy reportedly laughed and said, "Well, George, you're supposed to be one of the smartest guys in town, but you're crazier than hell. That will never happen."[1] By the time of the Tet offensive, as we have seen, more than 500,000 Americans were engaged in conflict in Vietnam.

George Ball and a few, very few, others in Washington tried to alert both Kennedy and Johnson to the dangers of intervention in a complex conflict in Asia, in which people of the same race were battling for power, but these men never succeeded in convincing the presidents they served that saving Vietnam would prove to be *too* costly, or that the considerable costs, moral and otherwise, of leaving might very well be less damaging than staying. So as the American commitment to keep South Vietnam from the communists persisted, the irony of the situation did not escape notice: The longer we persevered, the more lives were lost, and the more lives were lost, the greater the need to justify the cause. The most alarming aspect of it all was that as it became more and more important to justify the cause, the chances for outright success—for ousting the communists and securing the freedom of South Vietnam—seemed to become less and less.

As the war dragged on through the years of escalation, Vietnam became a kind of national nightmare, a challenge that sapped the lives and energies of the American people and offered in return only unanswered questions. By March 1968, it seemed that the president of the United States himself had become another casualty. For this masterful politician had seen his greatest dreams for America crushed by events far away on the battlefields and in the villages of Vietnam. As the complexity of the task before him became apparent, a discouraged president had confided to aide Bill Moyers that he felt "like a hitchhiker caught in a hailstorm on a Texas highway. I can't run. I can't hide. And I can't make it stop."[2]

What was it that caused Johnson to change course on that fateful last day of March 1968? The Tet offensive was of course part of it. But the cause for the shift went deeper. It had to do with a crisis not on the battlefield, but on the home front. America seemed to be falling apart. By early 1968, the stability of American society and its institutions was shakier than it had been since the Civil War in the 1860s. To understand the Vietnam War, then, we must examine the domestic crisis that the Vietnam War wrought.

One of the many ironies of the conflict in Vietnam is that as the president broadened the American commitment to save South Vietnam, the nation's elected leaders began for the first time to question seriously whether the war was really winnable at all. Congress had always supported military aid to Indochina in the 1950s, and it backed the various presidential administrations' policies there right up through the early 1960s. In 1964, Congress had passed the Tonkin Gulf Resolution, giving the president a free hand to conduct the war.

By early 1966, however, more and more congressmen and senators, sensing that all was not well, had begun to question the war and the Johnson administration's handling of it.

American citizens express their opinions about the war at a peace rally in Los Angeles, 1966. (Camera Press Ltd. photo.)

What lay behind the new zeal to question what was going on in Vietnam? Many things. First, President Johnson had not provided Americans with a clear enough picture of his approach to war. He seldom consulted with members of Congress, preferring to run the war from the White House, depending upon his personal advisers. Representative Gerald R. Ford of Michigan (later President Ford) was one of many congressmen who grew increasingly skeptical of the lack of congressional participation. Ford referred to Vietnam as "President Johnson's war," claiming that the president "plays everything too close to the vest."[3]

With each announced escalation and with rising American casualties, Congress wanted signs of progress. The trouble was that in the eyes of most of the men and women on Capitol Hill, progress meant a quick end to American involvement, not a war that would last years.

The full extent of congressional concern surfaced dramatically in February 1966, when the entire country witnessed the unusual spectacle of U.S. senators grilling Secretary of State Dean Rusk on television about Vietnam. While some senators criticized the president for imposing damaging restrictions on the military's effort to win, others questioned why the United States needed to be in Vietnam at all. In late 1965, questions had been raised as to whether or not Johnson had told the American people the whole truth about Hanoi's willingness to negotiate a settlement ending the fighting. Johnson had characterized the enemy as being inflexible, not interested in compromise. But some sources had evidence that Johnson had been the inflexible party. They pointed with anger to the president's refusal to halt the bombing to entice the North Vietnamese to the table.

Fear over the dire consequences of escalation had grown with each announcement of troop increases. Under heated questioning, Secretary Rusk pointed out that America's commitments, both to her allies and to her moral ideals, required that we persevere and challenge the aggression of the North Vietnamese, step by step. If the north stopped raising the stakes, so would the United States.

For their part, the senators felt that holding the line in Vietnam was rapidly reaching the point where the commitment was out of proportion to the strategic value of the country we were trying to defend. Rusk insisted that Vietnam was of critical value, a symbol of American resolve, but the senators were skeptical. Joseph Clark of Pennsylvania voiced the concern of many of his colleagues when he commented: ". . . I would hope very much that we are going to stop escalating this war any further. I think it was about a year ago that you told me . . . that we have lots of wiggle room. I think we are running out of wiggle room. I think we are coming pretty close to the point of no return, and personally I am scared to death we are on our way to nuclear World War Three."[4]

The Senate and House hearings exposed the country's Vietnam policy to a host of exceedingly difficult questions. It seemed to many, in Washington and throughout America, that the nation was being asked to sacrifice a great deal in order to save a people who hadn't demonstrated any great resolve to save themselves. In the eyes of men like Senator Clark, the risks of involvement were growing larger daily, while the chances for achieving our major goal—a free and independent South Vietnam—were diminishing. And yet the realities of politics left both the president and Congress in a tough, seemingly impossible situation. For no one was willing to support a quick—and immensely humiliating—exit from Vietnam. So despite congressional doubt, the war dragged on, and Lyndon Johnson continued to be the primary shaper of American policy.

While the administration forged ahead with its escalation, more Americans than ever before grew impatient, and the steadily growing murmurs of discontent became a major concern. A senior assistant to Robert McNamara, Alain Enthoven, analyzed the conflict ominously as "a race between, on the one hand, the development of a viable South Vietnam and, on the other, a gradual loss in public support"[5] for the war at home. Time would prove Enthoven's assessment to be a most perceptive one. Americans would not continue to support the venture in South Vietnam for much longer unless the meaning of the war could be made much clearer than it was in 1966.

Throughout 1966 and 1967, as the casualty lists grew longer and military operations more involved, the voices of dissent became more strident. The American churches were among the first institutions to challenge the American presence in Vietnam. William Sloane Coffin, the chaplain of Yale University and a well-known social activist, reported in 1966 that 150 Clergy Concerned About Vietnam committees had been formed in forty-three states. Many clergy were active in organizing demonstrations across the nation against the senseless brutality of the war. Thousands of concerned citizens gathered to hold overnight vigils in Chicago and New York. University scholars and other intellectuals began to suggest that Vietnam was breaking America apart at the seams. Many not only spoke against the war, but participated in "sit-ins" and marches to protest against America's presence in Vietnam.

This young girl carries a sign bearing a slogan that many American university students chanted during the war. (U.S. Army photo, courtesy Shelby L. Stanton.)

In February 1967, the dean of American historians, Henry Steele Commager, weighed in against U.S. policy in Vietnam, arguing persuasively that "we [Americans] do not have the resources—material, intellectual, or moral—to be at once an American power, a European power, and an Asian power."[6]

On October 16, 1967, 120 antiwar demonstrators were arrested after they staged a sit-in at the Oakland, California, draft induction center. A massive demonstration against the war took place in Washington on October 21, as the entire spectrum of antiwar activists—writers, students, pacificists, clergy, and even a few disillusioned Vietnam veterans—gathered together to march on the symbol of American military power, the Pentagon. It was a stirring, pas-

The big march on the pentagon. Military police, rifles raised, clash with the antiwar crowd. (U.S. Army photo, courtesy Shelby L. Stanton.)

sionate event. Violence erupted as antiwar demonstrators clashed with those who wanted America to stay on the course it had set for itself.

The march on the Pentagon was so large, so serious in the eyes of the government, that unusual security measures were taken. Troops of the Eighty-second Airborne Division, a crack U.S. Army unit, were called in to protect the Capitol. Troops were also stationed at the entrances to the Pentagon and White House. While the government was calling 30,000 men a month into the armed services, draft cards were burned in open defiance of the law. By the end of 1967, polls revealed that for the first time a majority of Americans believed the United States had been mistaken to intervene at all in Vietnam.

Moreover, the "credibility gap"—the gap between what the administration said about the war and what the people as a whole believed—was widening. Americans were no longer sure their government even knew what was going on in Vietnam. Nor were they sure whether they had been given accurate information about the issues involved. The American people did know that the killing went on, but more people than ever before refused to see high body counts as progress. Conservatives then believed, and still believe, that the press played a vital role in promoting the antiwar position, for better or for worse.

The collapse of confidence did not arise solely out of the administration's handling of things in Vietnam itself. To understand the passions of the antiwar movement in the United States, we must know something of the overall social and political atmosphere in America in the 1960s.

Now it is generally agreed that the 1960s were a decade of tumultuous change for America. The social landscape of the nation had been transformed, altered by a host of passions and concerns. This was the time of the civil rights movement. Americans of many races joined hands with blacks in the fight for equal justice. The crusade to rid America of its problems, both social and economic, to create a new order of things, to eliminate poverty in the richest nation on earth, had captured the imagination of idealistic young people across the country. Along with the black community and liberal intellectuals, students challenged the established order in America to address their grievances.

The emergence of the so-called counterculture, a diverse group of young Americans drawn together by a sense of hope and an idealistic vision of a world without violence, hatred, and prejudice, meshed with the causes of the civil rights and the antiwar movements, putting tremendous pressure on America's social fabric. Many members of the counterculture were committed to a spirit of rebellion. They dismissed the values of their parents and the established order as destructive and immoral.

As the 1960s moved forward, the concerns of all of these Americans seemed to converge on the war in Vietnam. In a time of social upheaval, when so much needed to be done at home, it seemed increasingly senseless for Americans to be fighting and dying on Asian battlefields. By 1967, Martin Luther King's civil rights crusade depicted the war in Vietnam as a senseless drain on scarce spiritual and economic resources better spent taking care of injustice and poverty at home. Vietnam became for many blacks and for many of America's young a kind of symbol of America's lack of spiritual direction, an evil and immoral undertaking. What made civil rights leaders even more bitter was that in the early years of the war, a disproportionate number of blacks saw combat in Vietnam and died there.

Not all Americans saw things this way, of course. But those who did not were nowhere near as vocal about their beliefs. Still, many blue-collar Americans, fearing that the world they knew was being threatened by forces they could not control, took to the streets in support of the government's war and of the way of life many in the counterculture dismissed as being out of touch with reality. So more violence resulted in the streets, and on the college campuses around the nation.

The ultimate effect of the antiwar movement, which would persist in its activities until the bitter end in 1973, remains one of the unsolved mysteries of America's long involvement in Vietnam. Surely the movement against the war succeeded in clarifying one thing: For many of America's younger generation, for the disadvantaged who could not escape the draft, the war seemed more and

Chicago police charge into a group of demonstrators in Grant Park. Violence was common at antiwar riots in the late 1960s. (AP/Wide World Photos.)

more a senseless episode conducted by a government out of touch with their concerns.

As time went on, the relationship between the halls of power in Washington and the people in the streets grew more bitter. Many of those in the antiwar movement who attacked the morality of the war, however, suffered from the same kind of stubborn blindness they criticized the government for exhibiting. Administration spokesmen who tried to explain that the position the United States found itself in was the result of commitments it could not in good faith just abandon were shouted off the stage, not even allowed to express their views. The antiwar activists believed the war was wrong and that it should be ended, but few of them had anything to say about how the United States could leave Vietnam without inflicting a disastrous wound upon its credibility around the world, or without encouraging communist revolution elsewhere. To simply leave after so much American blood had been spilled was unacceptable to the majority of Americans.

It is also true, as Colonel Harry G. Summers, Jr., one of America's most perceptive students of the war, has pointed out in his *Vietnam War Almanac*, that the most dramatic performances of those on the extreme side of the antiwar movement actually may have prolonged the war. Jane Fonda's donning of an NVA soldier's helmet, the burning of draft cards, and outrageous statements about U.S. soldiers committing genocide (systematic killing of an entire population) actually intensified many Americans' belief that we should continue fighting until we could truly defeat the North Vietnamese. To many conservative Americans, there was something morally wrong with abandoning the president during a time of national crisis.

Some have even called the actions of extreme antiwar activists treasonous, and not without justification. For we know with certainty that the North Vietnamese took heart from the statements and actions of America's antiwar spokespeople, just as such actions must have gravely disheartened the American soldiers fighting and dying in Vietnam. In fact, Hanoi was all along depending upon the American antiwar movement to help force an end to the American involvement.

The reader will have to make his or her own judgment on the morality of the antiwar movement's activities, but about one thing there is little doubt. It played a decisive role in exposing the flaws and ambiguities of the American effort in Vietnam, and therefore was a major force in bringing America's involvement in Southeast Asia to an end.

7. America's Enemy in Vietnam

Since success in war depends upon unflinching will, it makes sense for people fighting one another to paint the darkest, most grotesque picture possible of the enemy. For the will to win in any war is strengthened by the belief that the adversary, whoever he is, stands for the wrong things and fights in immoral ways. Moreover, hatred of the enemy motivates troops and propels support for war on the home front.

The American people, for the most part, did not think of the VC or the NVA with this kind of vehement hatred. To be sure, the "grunts"—foot soldiers—who stalked the mountains and jungles of Vietnam had their disparaging names for the communist troops. They were called "gooks," or "slopes," or "dinks." And, of course, American troops believed their enemy capable of the utmost ruthlessness. But both in the field and at home, the communists in Vietnam were not loathed with the same intensity as the Germans and Japanese were in World War II.

Americans did not hate the enemy. Nor, unfortunately, did they understand him. What held communist military units together even after staggering losses? What were the ideas that motivated the North Vietnamese to fight for so long and to defeat a great world power? Why were the Vietcong so much better at gaining control over the villages than the South Vietnamese government? In this chapter, we will provide an overview of the ideas and experiences of the people the Americans fought against in Vietnam, beginning with a discussion of the motivating ideas of Hanoi's leaders.

Ho Chi Minh, Le Duan, Vo Nguyen Giap, and the other major

133

Vietnamese communists were shrewd, dedicated proponents of Vietnamese nationalism. While they had all spent the better part of their lives in the quest for Vietnamese independence, they were equally committed to establishing a new political order in Vietnam through communist revolution. They had read Marx and Lenin, the fathers of communism. Many, including Ho, had been educated and trained in the subtleties of communist doctrine in Beijing and Moscow. And although during the war Hanoi went to great pains to deny it, a handful of professional revolutionaries in Hanoi ran the show entirely in South Vietnam. The indigenous force fighting the GVN in South Vietnam did not make its own decisions, but followed the dictates and doctrines established for it by the leadership in Hanoi.

Marxist-Leninist doctrine teaches that social justice can be achieved only by the rising up of the workers against the capitalists—those who own the means of production and all institutions of power. The ultimate goal of a communist society is the establishment of a classless society, in which all property is communally owned, and in which the state eventually disappears altogether, opening the way for all human beings to achieve their maximum potential without government interference. Marx wrote that social relationships should be governed according to the principle "From each according to his ability, to each according to his needs."

This is, of course, the theory. In practice, communist societies have encountered tremendous difficulties in trying to live up to the doctrine. The economic system associated with communist government, centralized planning, has proved woefully inefficient in meeting the needs of the people, and communist governments have found it impossible to share power with those who do not share their political values. Nonetheless, communism has been immensely appealing to poor and downtrodden peoples throughout the third world. Why?

First, it promises something all peoples want: freedom and independence from oppressors. In the waning days of the colonial empires, the peoples of the third world grew more and more aware of the usefulness of communist revolution as a tool for gaining independence from their colonial masters. Also, communist doctrine provides a strong, unifying set of beliefs and holds forth the vision of a kind of heaven on earth for all who wish to join the revolution. Through sacrifice and dedication to the Communist Party comes a life of freedom and glory, a chance for every man to make history.

This, in fact, is one of the grand themes running throughout all of communist Vietnamese literature. It is certainly the key message in General Giap's small book, *National Liberation War in Vietnam*, in which the general declares openly that *only the Communist Party* has the resources and knowledge to expel the Americans from Vietnamese soil. It alone has the moral power to drive a small nation to victory over the "international gendarme and number one enemy of mankind." It alone "has the revolutionary courage to resolutely lead the masses to stand up and break the yoke of the colonialists . . . to overcome all difficulties and hardships and defeat strong and fierce imperialist aggressors, including U.S. imperialists."[1] The party teaches the people, providing them with the wisdom and guidance they need to overcome the oppressors (the South Vietnamese government and the United States, in the party's eyes).

To most Americans the values of the communist political system are quite difficult to swallow, largely because there is so little room for individual initiative and expression. Under communist rule in Vietnam, the average villager has no real say in who governs his village. Individual initiative—working a side job to gain extra money for one's family, for instance—is frowned upon as putting one's own interests ahead of those of the state. And those interests are determined exclusively by the party elite; individuals are expected to obey the instructions of the party to the letter.

Dedicated followers of communism see things quite differently than do those who believe in Western-style democracy. To them, strict compliance with the dictates of the party is the best road to social justice. Only by working together, within the discipline of the party, is it possible for workers or peasants to move forward. And as one moves forward, *all* move forward.

Whatever its deficiencies, communism as a political idea had considerable appeal to many Vietnamese. It satisfied, at least initially, some of the needs of the Vietnamese conscience. The ideas were easier to comprehend than those of Western-style democracy, as they meshed more easily with the communal way of life that had evolved over the centuries in the villages. Communism provided many Vietnamese with a well-organized vehicle to obtain their independence, to rid their nation of all foreign "domination," and to participate in a worldwide movement—revolution against capitalism.

The strength of communism in Vietnam also grew from its effectiveness in stifling dissent and political opposition. The superior organizational skills of the Vietcong drove many American advisers to the brink of despair. When steady and persistent discussion of communist doctrine failed to win over the villagers in South Vietnam, the VC resorted to killing off the opposition or assassinating village chiefs just to make a point to the rest of the population. Political dissent was not tolerated.

Thus communism took hold in Vietnam not so much because the people had compared the ideas of Marx to those of Washington and Jefferson and found the ideas of the Americans lacking. Its success was due to the far greater ability of the communists to organize and control the peasantry, and to isolate them from dissenting information.

We turn our attention now to the type of forces and strategy Hanoi employed in its war against the Americans. The Vietcong were, of course, the men and women of South Vietnam who supported the revolution. It was they who carried out the guerrilla operations against the government of South Vietnam, its armed forces, and those of the United States. As a fighting force, they were far more active before 1968 than after, because the VC ranks were devastated by the Tet offensive. The VC had a political arm, the National Liberation Front, as mentioned earlier. During the war, the NLF was presented to the world as an independent political organization, with no ties to Hanoi other than friendship. Since the end of the war, however, the communist leaders of Vietnam have acknowledged that they were

The Vietnamese history-teacher-turned-general, Vo Nguyen Giap. (Camera Press Ltd. photo.)

in control of the NLF from the very beginning. It was the communist Lao Dong (Workers Party) in Hanoi which established the NLF's goals, organization, and strategy for the entire war.

The other major military force of America's adversary was the North Vietnamese Army. Unlike the VC, the NVA was a traditional armed force run by men who were professional soldiers. Throughout the Vietnam War, the NVA grew dramatically in size and fighting capacity. In 1964 it consisted of 250,000 men, organized into some fifteen divisions. It was essentially a lightly armed infantry-oriented army. By 1974, more than half a million men were in its ranks. World War II–vintage weapons had been replaced by modern automatic assault rifles, and a number of armored divisions (employing tanks and other heavy weaponry) had come into being.

For the North Vietnamese, unlike the Americans, the war in Vietnam required sacrifices of everyone. These civilians are making ammunition by hand. (U.S. Army photo.)

Two captured Vietcong are interrogated. (U.S. Army photo.)

We do not know as much as we would like to about the organization of the communist forces, but we do know that both the VC
and the NVA were highly motivated and well trained. They believed they could oust the Americans from Vietnam, despite the tremendous technological advantages and professionalism of the U.S.
forces, and this belief was reinforced again and again by both the
military and political leadership.

In pamphlets, books, and speeches, the men who commanded
the formidable communist military machine stressed the intimate
connection between Vietnam's long and glorious military history and
Marxist revolutionary thought.

In the struggle against the Americans and the "puppet" government in the south, General Giap stressed that the "resolution and
activity of all the people" would be required. To gain all-inclusive
power over as much territory as possible, the communist leadership
nurtured hundreds and hundreds of tightly knit groups called cells.
Each cell consisted of from three to twelve people, all of about the
same rank in the hierarchy. Each cell member knew of the activities

of only his cell. One—and only one—member of the cell would take orders directly from a member of a higher-level cell. In this fashion, village cells would receive orders from a particular district cell, which in turn would get its orders from a regional cell.

Not all cells were strictly military in nature. Some were designed to carry out propaganda functions; others taught the history of the communist party; still others organized village security operations. All cells were monitored by the party leadership to ensure that they performed correctly and followed through on their orders.

In the early 1960s, the tightly organized and dedicated VC cells

Vietnamese postage stamps commemorating the shooting down of U.S. planes. Today in Vietnam several downed B-52s remain where they fell, as reminders of the long war. (Courtesy Harry G. Summers, Jr.)

U.S. Air Force captain Wilmer N. Grubb, held at bayonet-point by an NVA soldier, is given first aid. (U.S. Air Force photo.)

were able to take control over one village after another right under the noses of government soldiers and officials. There was, of course, some variety in the techniques used to attain control. But basically it worked as follows:

First, members of a political education cell would try to win over an unsuspecting villager who held a prominent position in his community. A week or two following the initial contact, the communists might tell their contact in the village that they wanted to give a lecture or two on revolution to the people. In the lecture they would point out the failures of the government to provide them with what they needed. An atrocity story or two about ARVN troops would help to sway doubters. After a number of night visits, the communists would choose a few candidates for an election to a revolutionary village council. The council members would see to it that meetings took place to discuss village problems, and they might report to the VC on various events or activities relating to GVN activity in the area that the villagers had reported.

With the council in place, it was only a matter of time and consistent effort until the communists gained a stranglehold on the entire village. Taxes would be collected by a trusted villager assigned to the task. VC military units would come into the village at night, evading the daily patrols that were supposed to provide security against VC infiltration. If an influential villager refused to cooperate and began to work against the revolution, the VC might stage a trial, or in some cases an execution. The typical execution techniques were beheading or disembowelment. It was believed such gory methods were most effective in impressing the local population that the revolution was, after all, to be taken very seriously.

After the communists had the village under their thumb, a host of village organizations would be created. Farmers would be assigned to one revolutionary group. Old people and students would be required to meet to discuss their common problems and the role of the revolution in their lives. Soon, it would be impossible *not* to be a member of the revolution.

Was there any choice in all of this for the average Vietnamese rice farmer? Very little, in fact. It was not so much that the villagers of Vietnam chose the revolution as that the revolution chose them. The American writer Frances Fitzgerald describes the process this way in *Fire in the Lake*:

> Through their [the Viet Cong's] constant meetings, their private talks with the villagers, and their organization of collective work, they had established a network of personal contacts much more dense than the village had ever known. If only because they dared not break the balance of intelligence the villagers pro-

tected both the Front [NLF] and each other from the government troops. To the extent that they kept this trust, they increasingly boxed themselves into a series of obligations, one of which led to the other. . . . They might not have wholeheartedly supported the Front, but they were at least committed to it by occupation.[2]

More than anything else, it was the organizational skill of the Vietcong which threatened the collapse of the government in South Vietnam in the early 1960s. In the eyes of the communists themselves, their early success in South Vietnam was due more to *political* action, not military expertise. What the VC had done was prevent the government of South Vietnam from gaining and maintaining power in the basic unit of the Vietnamese nation—the village. That political action was important was hardly a surprise to the architects of communist war. General Giap himself, the preeminent military man in modern Vietnamese history, has written that political work provides the source of strength for fighting power.

In fact, political struggle was one of the two great elements in the strategy Hanoi devised to unify all of Vietnam under its control. That strategy, called *dau tranh* in Vietnamese (translated roughly as "struggle movement"), was a simple and amazingly effective approach to war against a great military power like the United States. It called for the careful coordination of *dau tranh vu tang* (armed struggle) with *dau tranh chinh tri* (political struggle). Depending on their own strengths and those of their enemy, the communists emphasized one element or the other. Early in the 1960s, as we have seen, the emphasis was on political struggle to weaken the South Vietnamese government. Between 1965 and 1968, the focus was on armed struggle.

Regardless of which aspect of the strategy was emphasized, the communists never lost sight of their ultimate objective, nor was their zeal diminished by the staggering losses they suffered when they tried to fight the Americans directly. It was above all else for the com-

Ho Chi Minh, the first and only president of communist Vietnam. (Camera Press Ltd. photo.)

munists a total war. The enemy, wrote General Giap, "can find no safe place in a war without a front line, no rear . . . but with an ubiquitous battlefield."[3]

Strategies, of course, are made by leaders. But what of the ordinary soldier, charged with the task of carrying out the strategy? We have seen that the North Vietnamese soldiers and the Vietcong were highly trained and motivated. They were also a very experienced fighting force. Many had fought in the jungle against the French for years before most Americans had entered the picture. The training went beyond military matters. Political education—teaching the meaning and the purpose of the revolution—played a vital role in maintaining the fighting edge of the troops.

Preparation and sacrifice are keys to success in any war. The Vietnamese communists were particularly conscious of the need for both. Training was continuous. Over the years, the communists developed an elaborate series of tunnels all over VC-held areas of South Vietnam. These underground mini-cities contained housing, hospitals, arsenals, food stores, and everything else required to fight a long, hard war. Most of the digging was done by hand. The number of man-hours it took to dig these tunnels—and there were hundreds of miles of them—is inestimable.

The fighting in Vietnam was done primarily by infantry units, which at one point or another had come down the Ho Chi Minh Trail through Laos and Cambodia into South Vietnam's battlegrounds. Coming down the trail was inevitably a harrowing experience. Many NVA soldiers died along the way, the victims of bombings, ambush, or sickness contracted in the jungle. NVA Second Lieutenant Tran Xuan Meim came down the trail in the mid-1960s. He offered this account in an excellent book titled *Portrait of the Enemy* by David Chanoff and Doan Van Toai:

> At places along the side of the trail were the hulks of
> military vehicles and graves, graves of NVA soldiers.
> They were arranged neatly and had the names and

American troops discover the main entrance to a Vietcong tunnel complex.
(U.S. Army photo.)

dates of death inscribed on them. . . . Inside, I was
sure that everyone was frightened. But nobody said a
word about it.

On the section of the trail going toward Kontum
every day we saw groups of wounded soldiers coming
home. When we exchanged a few words they told us,
"You'll see all kinds of pleasures in the south." The
ones who were marching had mutilated arms. Those
who had lost their legs were carried [by trucks] under
camouflage. Some of them had been burned by napalm. Others were deformed or blind. We used to say
to each other, "On arrival in the south try to keep
your faces intact."[4]

The journey to the south has become part of communist Vietnam's sacred folklore. Those who made the trek, whether they survived American bombing or ambush or not, are seen as brave heroes
of the revolution.

Wherever the communists fought—on the trail, in the central
highlands, or in South Vietnamese cities—their performance was by
most accounts quite good. When confronted with heavy American
firepower, the favored approach was hit-and-run. But frontal assaults on isolated fire bases were also common. More often than not,
these human-wave attacks resulted in very heavy casualties. But
except in the Tet offensive of 1968, the losses were never heavy enough
to shake the morale of the army or its commanders for long.

One of the enduring myths of the war in Vietnam has been that
the enemy had little or no power in comparison to the mighty United
States. The vast difference in size and industrial development of the
two nations lent credence to the myth. In reality, the advantages
the communists enjoyed in waging war against a superpower like
the United States were considerable. On the battlefield, the communists had more experienced fighters, men who for years had fought

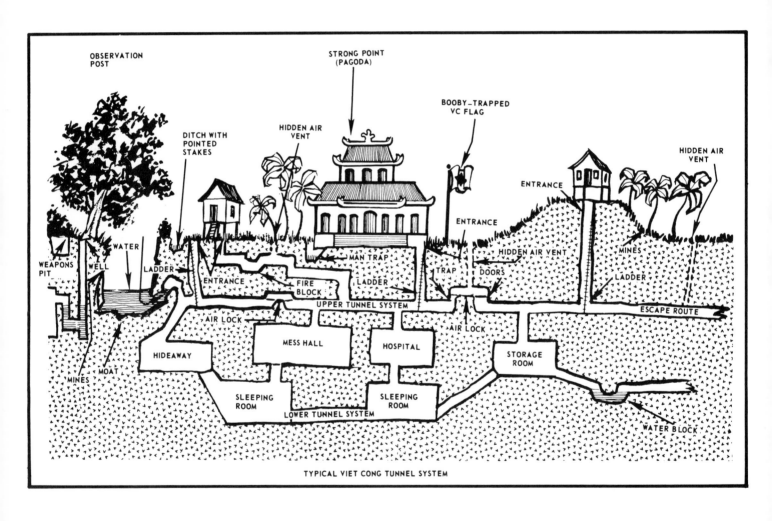

A typical Vietcong fortified village. (Source: LTC Albert N. Garland, ed., *Infantry in Vietnam* [Fort Benning, Georgia; *Infantry* Magazine, 1967], 242.)

in the jungles and mountains. In Cambodia and Laos, communist forces were allowed to retreat without fear of harassment for many years. The Rules of Engagement—a set of strict limitations on where and how allied forces could fight the enemy—prohibited Americans and South Vietnamese from chasing them as they fled to their sanctuaries.

On the political front—so crucial to carrying on a war—the United States had to worry about public judgments of its policy. The communists did not. They controlled the flow of information, and public dissent was not tolerated.

The greatest advantage the communists had was their unbending will. They were willing to sacrifice millions of lives to achieve their objective. It simply did not matter how many men were killed. All that was important was that they oust the Americans, crush the GVN, and gain control over South Vietnam. Perhaps the greatest example of Hanoi's ruthlessness unfolds later on in our story, after the Americans had left and the South Vietnamese had been vanquished. Then the Vietcong leaders, their people and their political interests as southerners, were no longer important to the North Vietnamese. Soon the northerners forced the Vietcong out of positions of influence and power.

Truong Nhu Trang, minister of social justice for the Vietcong, has written memorably of Hanoi's betrayal of southern communists in his book *A Viet Cong Memoir*. Not long after communist victory had been achieved, it dawned upon the Vietcong that the goal of the North Vietnamese was, and always had been, the creation of a totalitarian state "in which the traditions and cultures of the south would be ground and molded by the political machine of the conquerors."[5] But before this betrayal, several years of bloody war lay ahead, and there was a new American president, Richard M. Nixon, to deal with. In January 1969, an entirely new phase of war in Vietnam was about to begin.

8. President Nixon's War: Peace with Honor?

With the Nixon administration's assumption of power in January 1969, America's war in Vietnam took on an entirely new coloration. The administrations of Kennedy and Johnson had made the fateful decisions committing America to defend Vietnam. Now a new group of men, Republicans for the most part, would be running the show.

Under Richard M. Nixon, the contradictions and ambiguities of American involvement which had become apparent following the Tet offensive came more painfully into view. In the new American president the Vietnamese communists found an adversary whose will was as steadfast and unyielding as their own. Unlike Johnson, Nixon had ample experience in foreign policy—it was, in fact, his major interest—and he was a shrewd strategist. He knew that an all-out military victory in Vietnam was impossible, given the domestic turmoil and the limitations the United States had imposed upon its war effort. And so Nixon sought "peace with honor" in Vietnam. That meant that the United States would extricate itself from the war in a way that would not be read by the world as an outright defeat for the United States. South Vietnam, whose survival the war was being fought for, would not be abandoned, but the American role would have to return to one of advice and support.

Ending the war honorably, believed Henry Kissinger, the former Harvard professor who was the main architect of Nixon's strategy, was essential not only for the people of Vietnam but for the security of the entire world. If the United States simply got up and left, its credibility as a nation willing to fight for freedom would disinte-

150

President Richard M. Nixon waves to the crowd. (U.S. Army photo.)

grate. That meant that free peoples everywhere would be in danger. For men with ambitions of leading America into a more prominent role in world affairs, this was an unthinkable disaster. Both the president and Kissinger were ready to do just about anything to prevent it from happening.

Clinging tenaciously to his objective, Nixon presided over the most complicated and debatable of wars for four years. For the American military, it was a time of disengagement—American troops would withdraw, slowly but surely, from the quagmire. But the disengagement would be punctuated by periodic explosions of American military might. As we shall see, precisely at the time when the public was growing more and more anxious about the nightmare of Vietnam, Nixon chose to *widen* the war, to expand the territory upon which the troops fought, in order to show the North Vietnamese and their Soviet and Chinese allies that the United States of America wasn't about to settle matters on their terms, no matter how unpopular the war was at home.

The troops in Indochina during the last four years of America's Vietnam war fought on with the knowledge that all-out victory was no longer the objective. They were there, rather, to keep the enemy from tightening the noose he had already managed to throw around the neck of South Vietnam. The U.S. military also provided Richard Nixon and Henry Kissinger with much-needed leverage to bargain for an honorable peace.

In the end, Nixon would put an end to America's long and tragic involvement in Vietnam. In the process of doing so, however, his presidency would be savaged, and he would be personally disgraced. Soon after America's last combat troops left Vietnam, Nixon would become the first and only American president to resign from office. The major reason for his fall from grace came down to a single word: Vietnam.

The new administration's mission to obtain peace with honor began with a bold and unexpected step: The president approved

General Earle Wheeler's plan to bomb the Cambodian sanctuaries of the communists.

Cambodia had for years remained neutral in the war of its neighbor, at least officially. The Vietnamese communists, both Vietcong and NVA, had always used the sparsely populated jungles just across the border from Vietnam as staging areas for operations, and more importantly, the trails and roads they constructed there formed part of the lifeline of revolution in South Vietnam—the Ho Chi Minh Trail.

The purpose of the bombing was to limit North Vietnam's ability to prey upon American forces, whose strength in numbers was steadily diminishing. Operation Menu, as the bombing was called, had other purposes as well. Soon after assuming office, Nixon had informed Hanoi through French intermediaries that he was ready to talk peace in Vietnam, and that a good first step would be a mutual withdrawal of American and North Vietnamese troops from South Vietnam. The Cambodian bombing was designed to show Hanoi that the United States was prepared to take harsh, effective military action in order to bring Hanoi around to serious negotiations. America would not consent to the elimination of the Thieu government as a precondition for negotiations.

For fourteen months, starting in March 1969, B-52 bombers dropped their deadly payloads down upon the sanctuaries, opening up what some have called a "secret war." Neither side was willing to go public on the Cambodian action, as neither wanted to be accused by the world of violating Cambodian territory. When the story of the bombing finally surfaced in 1973, it caused a sensation, leading to serious questions about the Nixon administration's reluctance to share its policies and methods with Congress or the people.

In May 1969, as the B-52s ravaged the Cambodian countryside, American ground troops fought one of the most bloody, ferocious engagements of the entire war. The objective of the Americans who fought this battle near the Laotian border, just west of the A Shau Valley, was to capture the Apbia mountain from the NVA troops

A B-52 Stratofortress in flight over Vietnam. (U.S. Air Force photo.)

who were firmly entrenched there. For ten days American troops, supported by artillery and jets, attempted to wrest the jungle-covered slopes of the mountain from the NVA. But the well-trained enemy had constructed bunkers that were virtually impossible to knock out with artillery or air power, so the American infantry had to take the hill through costly frontal assaults. Casualties were extremely high. After several attempts, the hill was captured.

Hamburger Hill, as the battle is now known, became famous as a symbol of the futility of traditional military success in Vietnam. The hill was abandoned by Americans the day after its capture. When *Life* magazine published the pictures of 241 men who had been killed during one week in Vietnam soon after the battle of Apbia, it set off a new storm of questioning and protest over America's involvement in Vietnam. Why had so many died for a piece of ground not worth even holding on to?

While the president and his advisers sought peace with honor, the toll in human suffering for America mounted at an alarming pace. In 1969 alone, almost 10,000 U.S. soldiers were killed in action. Nixon, and indeed most observers of the war, knew that the

American public would not continue to support U.S. policy in Vietnam if heavy casualties continued for long. If peace with honor was ever to be obtained, it would be necessary for the South Vietnamese armed forces to assume a larger role in fighting the enemy and providing security. The policy the Nixon administration devised became known as "Vietnamization." American aid and equipment would be provided for the local militia, and U.S. advisers would redouble their efforts to create a truly independent and effective South Vietnamese army.

Many of the civilian specialists on the Vietnam War in the Department of Defense had as early as 1967 called for new emphasis upon pacification programs, and the Nixon administration supported the idea. And so the CIA, recognizing the importance of reducing VC control over the peasantry, initiated the Phoenix program. A successful, if controversial, operation, Phoenix sought to integrate the intelligence-gathering organizations of the American military, the CIA, and the South Vietnamese in order to expose the Vietcong organizational structure in South Vietnam and root it out with highly trained military specialists. Some 6,000 Vietcong officials were eliminated through the Phoenix program, and the Vietcong, fearful of having their entire structure of power in the villages crumble, mounted a worldwide propaganda campaign against Phoenix, claiming that it was little more than an assassination bureau.

The Cambodian bombings, stepped-up pacification programs, and strenuous diplomatic efforts bought more time to shore up the South Vietnamese government and armed forces, but did not alter North Vietnam's position on a peace settlement. Hanoi remained firm in its insistence that the United States must withdraw all its troops before a settlement could become a reality.

This neither Kissinger nor Nixon found acceptable. As the administration pondered the situation in Vietnam in early 1970, it became apparent that a major military move would be needed to prevent North Vietnam from taking advantage of the shrinking American presence on the ground. Despite awareness of the public

U.S. troops train South Vietnamese soldiers in Nha Trang. (U.S. Army photo, courtesy Shelby L. Stanton.)

Pacification efforts were stepped up after Nixon became president. (Army News Features, courtesy Shelby L. Stanton.)

outcry a thrust into Cambodia by ground troops was likely to make, the decision was made to proceed. The president took his case right to the American people, announcing in a nationally televised speech on April 30 that he had decided to go to "the heart of the trouble" and clean out the entrenched positions and supply bases North Vietnam had in the remote region. Some of the positions, the president correctly pointed out, were as close to Saigon as Baltimore was to Washington, D.C.

The reaction in the United States to the news of the "Cambodian incursion," as the president called it, was calamitous. Antiwar demonstrations broke out with renewed intensity, resulting in tragic violence. At Kent State University in Ohio, on May 4, jittery Na-

Melvin Laird, Nixon's secretary of defense. Laird, believing that America had had enough of Vietnam, pressed hard to make sure that troops were withdrawn on schedule. (Courtesy Shelby L. Stanton.)

tional Guardsmen, on the campus to keep order, fired into the crowd, killing four demonstrators.

The nationwide protests seemed to make the president and Kissinger more determined than ever to conduct the war in Vietnam in secret in order to avoid the pressures of the State Department bureaucracy and of Congress, which more and more reflected the people's disillusionment with fighting in Vietnam at all. By all accounts, Richard M. Nixon was a man who thrived on crisis. As the furor over Vietnam grew, he stiffened his resolve to avoid what many clamored for—a quick, one-sided withdrawal that would be, in effect, an American surrender. Nixon pressed on, believing that through diplomatic and military pressure, he could find the North Vietnamese "breaking point."

But North Vietnam's breaking point was frustratingly difficult to find. The Cambodian incursion, like the American actions of 1969, only perpetuated stalemate on the battlefield. Hanoi's position on U.S. withdrawal stood.

In November and December 1970, American intelligence sources reported that the North Vietnamese were sending large quantities of military supplies into Laos and Cambodia. Again the president responded with a show of military force, initiating a large-scale ground operation in Laos and heavy bombing of the Ho Chi Minh Trail, Hanoi, and Haiphong, where there were docks and shipyards.

The thrust into Laos, conducted almost exclusively by the ARVN, was to capture the town of Tchepone, a major enemy supply center. The South Vietnamese eventually got to their destination, but not before two of their battalions were completely overrun.

Back in the United States, the operation in Laos brought vehement protest in Congress. How could we be seeking peace if we were deliberately expanding the battlefield in Indochina? Senator J. William Fulbright called for the repeal of the Tonkin Gulf Resolution. He went so far as to advocate that Congress pass legislation making it illegal for the president to initiate such military ventures in Indochina without congressional approval. In April 1970, yet another round of antiwar protests took place across the nation.

In the late spring of 1971, as the war dragged on, a former government defense analyst who had worked for Robert McNamara, Daniel Ellsberg, gave to the *New York Times* a copy of a secret study of the war Lyndon Johnson had ordered compiled. Ellsberg himself had participated in the writing of the study, and its publication, which began in June 1971 in the *Times*, created an uproar. The study was called *The History of the U.S. Decision Making Process on Vietnam*, but it became known to the world simply as the Pentagon Papers.

The study documented the reservations and doubts of many of the key decision-makers and their advisers about America's policies in Vietnam, and it left the American public believing that the government had been hiding the full story of the war. The president was infuriated at its publication. It compromised the intelligence-gathering process in Vietnam itself, widened the credibility gap between the U.S. government and its people, and thereby decreased

This enemy equipment was captured by ARVN troops in Laos in 1971. (U.S. Army photo.)

U.S. ability to bargain with the North Vietnamese. A man with a penchant for secrecy, Nixon ordered the creation of a "plumbers" unit to find those who leaked classified information to journalists. It was an order that would come to haunt the president in due course.

The furor over the Pentagon Papers heightened Nixon's fear that the antiwar activists and the press were out to sabotage his efforts to end the war in a way that would not dishonor America. The president's bitterness fed his determination to move forward, no matter what obstacles stood in the way. And the obstacles, unfortunately, seemed greater than ever.

By the summer of 1971, more than half of all Americans believed that the United States had been mistaken to fight in Vietnam at all. According to one poll, 58 percent of the public believed the war immoral. Far fewer—31 percent—approved of President Nixon's handling of the war.

The lack of public support had profound consequences for the

American troops in the field. Without the clear objective of victory, their goal became simple survival. What mattered most to American soldiers in the latter years of the war was simply getting through their twelve or thirteen months of Vietnam duty. Any army which lacks popular support at home for its battlefield sacrifices suffers from morale problems, and there is little doubt that the Americans in Vietnam during President Nixon's tenure had serious problems.

Incidents of "fragging"—the deliberate killing of officers by their men to avoid dangerous action—increased markedly during this period. So did drug abuse. Drugs became a very serious problem for all the services, particularly the Army and Marine Corps. Marijuana, heroin, and opium were easy to obtain, and many soldiers turned to them as a way to escape the horrors of the war.

As time went on, it became increasingly difficult for the services to fill the ranks in Vietnam with qualified people. The rotation system damaged unit cohesion, compounding the problems of fighting without clear objectives. "Once America began to pull its troops out of Vietnam," Shelby Stanton writes in *The Rise and Fall of an American Army*, ". . . the average soldier simply wanted to get home alive and cared little for the ultimate fate of his formation [unit] or the accomplishment of the country's mission."[1]

The image of America's fighting men had by 1971 been in steady decline. Nothing damaged that image more than the infamous My Lai massacre, which occurred in March 1968 but wasn't revealed to the U.S. Army brass until 1969. An inexperienced and underqualified lieutenant, William Calley, had moved his twenty-five-man platoon into the hamlet of My Lai in Quang Ngai Province, gathered together some 150 villagers—old men, women, and children—and gunned them down. The My Lai incident gave the American public the impression—the mistaken impression—that this sort of thing happened all the time in Vietnam.

As the stalemate continued in South Vietnam, in early 1972, Hanoi was planning to go on the offensive once again, after a period of relatively reduced military activity. Hanoi's plan called for a

A Special Forces reconnaissance patrol prepares to be extracted by helicopter from the Ho Chi Minh Trail area in Laos, 1972. U.S. Army Special Forces officer Shelby L. Stanton commanded Thai troops on the mission. (Courtesy Shelby L. Stanton.)

massive, three-pronged attack from bases in Laos and North Vietnam. More than 120,000 troops would participate, making it the biggest communist operation since Tet.

The so-called Eastertide offensive began well for the North Vietnamese, as they overran many ARVN strongholds in Quang Tri Province soon after initiating attacks on March 30. Farther south, the ARVN fared no better, as the NVA poured into the central highlands from its bases in Laos. Several ARVN generals had to be relieved of their command on the battlefield for incompetence, cowardice, or both. It seemed that perhaps the NVA was correct in believing that without the help of U.S. ground troops, almost all of whom had left the country by this point, South Vietnam could be easily occupied. But the Americans shared some of the blame for the poor performance, as U.S. intelligence units failed to anticipate the scope of the invasion.

President Nixon showed little hesitation upon learning of the deteriorating situation in South Vietnam following the communist onslaught. He ordered massive B-52 strikes not only on the advancing columns of NVA troops and their bases, but also on the fuel depots in Hanoi and Haiphong. The enemy was forced to withdraw from the newly captured territory.

The offensive was a military defeat for Hanoi. It failed in its ultimate objective—overrunning South Vietnam. And yet, as was frequently the case in this complex war, North Vietnam's failure could not be read as a real victory for South Vietnam. The performance of the ARVN unnerved American military men on the scene. Some units had performed well, but no one really believed that the offensive could have been halted without overwhelming American airpower. And this was a great problem for the administration, which knew that American congressmen would be increasingly reluctant to provide the funds to bail out the South Vietnamese now that four-fifths of their own troops had been withdrawn.

Soon after the offensive, both the United States and Hanoi, weary of war, showed signs of willingness to compromise at the bargaining table. For their part, the North Vietnamese had seen enough of Richard Nixon to realize that this American president, a man reportedly obsessed with the idea of blowing North Vietnam to bits, wasn't going to settle matters exclusively on their terms.

Official talks had been taking place on and off in Paris since May 1968, but had achieved little. Now, in May 1971, Henry Kissinger, the mastermind of the American negotiating team, met with North Vietnam's chief negotiator, Le Duc Tho, at a private home near Paris. For the first time Kissinger suggested that a complete U.S. withdrawal might possibly take place within six months of an agreement to return U.S. prisoners. Kissinger made no mention, as he had in the past, of a complete withdrawal of NVA troops in exchange.

Tho found this a step in the right direction, but talks bogged down over whether the Thieu government should remain intact. The North Vietnamese insisted upon a coalition government in which the National Liberation Front would be represented. This had always been tantamount to surrender to the United States, and neither Kissinger nor Nixon would hear of it.

Believing that at this point Hanoi was unlikely to respond to yet another show of U.S. military might, Nixon and Kissinger attempted to apply a different sort of pressure on their adversary by exploiting the mounting tension between Hanoi's partners in revolution, China and the Soviet Union.

Ever since the Americans had arrived in force on the battlefield, the support of the world's most powerful communist countries had been necessary to keep the engines of war running in Hanoi. A country as poor as North Vietnam couldn't have kept its troops supplied with weapons, food, and ammunition without it. Political solidarity was important as well.

By the early 1970s, unfortunately for the North Vietnamese, the Chinese and Soviets were all but at each other's throats. The Chinese refused to let Soviet aircraft bearing supplies for the Vietnamese war effort fly over their territory. Soviet and Chinese border troops clashed on a number of occasions. As the two countries vied for power and prestige among the world's communist nations, good relations with the United States suddenly became a high priority.

Richard Nixon had made his political career as a hardline anticommunist. But neither he nor Kissinger would let their ideological differences with the two giants stand in the way of creating a more secure international order in which the United States would play the major role. In fact, since Nixon's assumption of the presidency, a major goal of his administration had been a thawing out of the cold war, of which Vietnam was but one tragic part. Nixon and Kissinger resolved to pressure North Vietnam by holding out promises of increased trade and warmer relations with America to China and the Soviet Union.

In February 1972 the president's overtures to China paid off with a highly publicized trip to Beijing. The resolution of the war in Vietnam was high on the agenda of the meetings between Nixon and Premier Zhou Enlai. The Chinese leader promised nothing concrete, but when Nixon announced a naval blockade of North Vietnam and the mining of Haiphong harbor, Zhou said nothing—an ominous signal to Hanoi. The Nixon administration had made it clear to Leonid Brezhnev, the leader of the Soviet Union, that it would be to his advantage to help resolve the conflict in a way that America could live with. Despite the blockade and harbor minings, things which earlier in the war would have resulted in harsh Soviet denunciations, little was heard from Moscow.

The declining enthusiasm of the Soviet Union and China for the war was but one of many reasons that the Americans and the North Vietnamese came close to establishing a peace in the fall of 1972. The Nixon administration by this time recognized that America's leverage was shrinking. The American people simply would not condone a new expanded American role should the North Vietnamese mount another major attack. The administration's military adventures over the past three years had demonstrated that the North Vietnamese were willing to take staggering losses and continue to fight on indefinitely, while the South Vietnamese clearly were not.

As the American presidential election of 1972 approached, both Henry Kissinger and Le Duc Tho were resolved to reach a settlement. On October 8, after three weeks of exhausting negotiations which had been punctuated by explosions of anger and frustration on both sides, a breakthrough occurred.

The tentative agreement required compromises by both sides. The United States for the first time openly stated that it would no longer insist upon the complete withdrawal of the North Vietnamese from their positions in South Vietnam. Whoever controlled territory at the time of the cease-fire would continue to hold it until a more complete political settlement could be obtained. Some called this a "leopard spot" arrangement, in which there would be pockets, or spots, of communist control within South Vietnam itself. The

North Vietnamese no longer insisted upon ousting the Thieu regime, and they agreed to release America's POWs, some of whom had been held captive for more than seven years.

But the really thorny issue—the political fate of South Vietnam—was simply ignored. It was agreed that a vaguely described "national council of reconciliation," consisting of representatives from the Vietcong, Thieu's government, and neutral countries, would supervise elections and see to it that peace prevailed.

Henry Kissinger announced that peace was at hand, but his statement proved to be a bit premature. President Thieu, who had little to gain by an agreement that left his government in political limbo and threatened by NVA troops on his own soil, was outraged when Kissinger presented the deal to him.

President Nixon considered it essential for Thieu to assent to an agreement which was supposed to represent "peace with honor." If the leader of the GVN didn't go along with the arrangement, it would appear that the United States was simply cutting its losses and running. The quest for a settlement stalled. Secret negotiations—without the representatives of South Vietnam—resumed in November, but the anger and distrust on both sides inhibited progress. By mid-December, talks broke off again.

Now it was time for Richard Nixon to take action. First he ordered that $1 billion in military hardware be sent to Vietnam to shore up the already huge military establishment. He warned Thieu that unless he stopped his complaints about the U.S. government's failure to defend his interests, further aid would be cut off. Nixon also instructed Admiral Thomas Moorer, chairman of the Joint Chiefs of Staff, to plan for a new round of bombing, saying, according to his own memoirs, "This is your chance to use military power to win this war, and if you don't, I'll consider you responsible."[2] Starting on December 18, 1972, Air Force and Navy fighter-bombers, along with B-52s, flew 1,700 sorties over Hanoi in eleven days, inflicting heavy damage upon the city's factories, power plants, and transportation network, but taking heavy losses themselves.

The reaction across America to the "Christmas bombing" was one of dismay and horror. Part of the reason for this was that the antiwar movement greatly exaggerated the civilian casualties such bombings inflicted, comparing the raids to those made on German and Japanese cities in World War II. More significantly, however, Americans felt that their president had embarked on yet another phase of a war no one in America wanted to fight any longer.

It wasn't long after the bombings that North Vietnam agreed to return to the negotiations. This time, at long last, an agreement was reached. Except for some minor changes, the terms were similar to those Thieu had scorned in October. Why had he now consented? He had received a personal letter from Richard Nixon assuring him that the United States would not desert his government should North

A reconnaissance photograph of a surface-to-air missile site in North Vietnam. The missiles brought down many American planes. (U.S. Air Force photo.)

At the conference table in Paris, January 13, 1973. (Camera Press Ltd. photo.)

Vietnam fail to respect the cease-fire agreement. In fact, though, Thieu had little choice. Nixon, most historians agree, was ready to sign the agreement to end American involvement in the Vietnam war without his old ally's blessing.

The agreement ending America's longest war, officially entitled "Agreement on Ending the War and Restoring the Peace in Vietnam," was signed on January 27, 1973, in Paris. While the agreement ended U.S. participation in hostilities in Southeast Asia, few believed it would end the fighting among the Vietnamese themselves. Thieu pressed on almost immediately to crush communist strongholds in the south. The North Vietnamese began to build an all-weather road down the Ho Chi Minh Trail, running from Quang Tri Province to the Mekong Delta, and an oil pipeline as well. The road and pipeline were designed, of course, to sustain a massive invasion of South Vietnam, an invasion far bigger than the Eastertide offensive of 1972.

The Nixon administration claimed to have achieved what it had sought: peace with honor. But the meaning of the agreement was not so clear to those who read the text of the document in the American papers the day after it was signed. The U.S. involvement on the ground would soon be over, but few doubted that if a crisis emerged, the president would do all in his power to prevent communist victory.

In a very real way, the Paris agreement ended only a chapter in the American story. American influence, the signs of American power, remained in South Vietnam. The last U.S. combat troops departed from Vietnamese soil in March 1973. But 9,000 or so "civilian" American advisers remained in the country, most of them employed officially by the government of South Vietnam. Many of these men were in fact recently retired U.S. servicemen.

Relations between the United States and Hanoi remained bitter. Years of war fostered distrust, and neither side believed its adversary would adhere to the letter of the agreement. Soon the North Vietnamese would denounce America for failing to follow through on its promises to provide $4.35 billion in aid. Nixon, determined to support his old ally, did everything possible to shore up the Thieu regime, threatening and cajoling Hanoi and providing the GVN with huge quantities of American military equipment.

Until the end of the Nixon presidency in August 1974, Kissinger and Nixon pressed for support of the GVN. Had the Watergate scandal not caused Nixon's resignation, it is quite likely such support would have persisted.

But Watergate had itself been prompted by the administration's policies in Vietnam. And when the communists initiated their mas-

April 1973: Vietcong prisoners await transportation to Hanoi in a prisoner exchange. (U.S. Marine Corps photo.)

sive blitzkrieg in the spring of 1975, Watergate had obliterated any possibility that the United States of America would rescue its old and unreliable ally, the Republic of Vietnam. No one, least of all the Congress of the United States, felt compelled to stick by President Nixon's promise to Thieu to save the day, once again, in Vietnam. South Vietnam was on its own.

9. The Fall and Its Legacies

The Paris agreement did not bring about a complete disengagement of the United States from Vietnam. It did mark the end of our direct combat involvement, and that was something which many in the United States were thankful for. For South Vietnam, however, the peace agreement was nothing more than a very short-lived cease-fire. The goals and objectives of both the Thieu regime and Hanoi were the same in mid-1973 as they had been in 1970 or 1968. The momentum in this new phase of war in Vietnam belonged decidedly to the communists.

The exit of the Americans had given communist forces a boost in morale, strengthening their will to pursue their objective. It had done just the opposite for the South Vietnamese government. Thieu had believed in Nixon's secret promise to come to his aid should Hanoi threaten to overrun his country. The Watergate investigations in Washington were every day diminishing the president's power to bargain in Congress and to assert his will in matters of foreign policy. The Indochina military adventures of Nixon and Kissinger contributed to the decline in trust of the executive branch. Congress was so bitter about Nixon's policies that it resorted to the power of the purse to tie its hands. On July 1, 1973, the Fulbright-Aiken Amendment became law. The intent of the document was plain enough:

> Notwithstanding any other provision of law, on or after August 15, 1973, no funds herein or heretofore appropriated may be obligated or expended to finance di-

171

rectly or indirectly combat activities by United States
military forces in or over or from off the shores of North
Vietnam, South Vietnam, Laos or Cambodia.[1]

Throughout the year, Congress hammered away at the president's power to use military force of any kind in Indochina. With
President Nixon's hands tied and with strong popular sentiment in
favor of complete extrication from Vietnam, Thieu, Ky, and other
South Vietnamese must have sensed that their days were numbered.
The signs of decay and imminent disaster were everywhere. The
withdrawal of American forces, with their tremendous spending
power, had crushed what little vitality was left in the South Vietnamese economy. Direct aid from the United States dropped from
well over $2 billion in 1973 to about $1 billion in 1974. The aid cuts
only heightened the desperation of a troubled people and sent Saigon reeling into yet another period of political intrigue and chaos.
For the ARVN, the aid cuts served as a kind of death sentence. They
had been trained to fight an American-style war. Now they would
have to do it without American money.

All of this was very good news to the determined, well-prepared
enemy to the north, which by late 1974 was planning a large-scale
invasion of South Vietnam. The final offensive of the Second Indochina War began in January 1975 with the quick capture of Phuoc
Long Province, the southern border of which lies but fifty miles north
of Saigon. The attack had been met with only token resistance, and
it proved what General Van Tien Dung, commander of the communist forces, had thought all along: that the American presidency had
been too weakened for the United States to respond with air power.
The North Vietnamese pressed forward, determined to see their plan
through to the end.

In early March, the communists began their drive into the cen-
tral highlands. Three divisions attacked Ban Me Thuot. President
Thieu ordered ARVN units in the highlands to retreat back toward
Saigon. Unfortunately, the general in command opted to fly himself

A meeting of the Four Party Joint Military Team in Hanoi in 1974. The Viet-cong, the North Vietnamese, the GVN, and the United States each had a delegation. The team was charged with the responsibility of supervising the cease-fire and resolving the problem of soldiers missing in action, among other things. (U.S. Army photo.)

out of the picture altogether, leaving his troops leaderless and in disarray.

In the critical middle region of South Vietnam, ARVN soldiers deserted their units *en masse* in an effort to find their families and take them to safety on the coast. More than 50,000 soldiers and 400,000 refugees began a trek down Route 7B, an old, infrequently used highway badly in need of repair. All the way to the coast, the column was shelled by NVA artillery. Thousands perished before reaching the coastal cities.

By the end of March, the communists had launched another prong of their blitzkrieg, moving infantry, tanks, and artillery across the DMZ, then heading south toward Da Nang. Again, ARVN units, undermanned and poorly led, disintegrated.

As one province after another succumbed to the North Vietnamese onslaught, President Thieu grew more embittered. He seldom left the confines of the lavish presidential palace. He seemed to those around him to be paralyzed by the greatest crisis in his nation's history, as if the pain of a country in ruins was just too much for him to face. At times he even refused to take urgent calls from his field commanders.

In Thieu's eyes, the tragedy unfolding before him had been caused neither by his own failings nor by the military incompetence of his generals. The Americans were to blame for failing to follow through on promises made when the peace accords had been signed.

While Thieu railed about his betrayers at the palace, the two men who bore the responsibility for evacuating the remaining Americans and their Vietnamese allies, Henry Kissinger and Ambassador Graham Martin, were busy planning the final exodus. It was a matter of the utmost delicacy: If the word from Washington to pull out came too quickly, there was a good chance panic would ensue, resulting in a bloodbath of unthinkable proportions. On the other hand, if the evacuation was not begun soon, chaos would result from a desperate, last-minute run on Tan Son Nhut airport and the U.S. embassy.

On April 17, Kissinger sent a top-secret cable to Martin:

WE HAVE JUST COMPLETED AN INTERAGENCY
REVIEW OF THE STATE OF PLAY IN SOUTH VIET-
NAM. YOU SHOULD KNOW THAT AT THE WSAG
[Washington Special Action Group] MEETING TO-
DAY THERE WAS ALMOST NO SUPPORT FOR THE
EVACUATION OF VIETNAMESE, AND FOR THE USE
OF AMERICAN FORCE TO HELP PROTECT ANY
EVACUATION. THE SENTIMENT OF OUR MILI-
TARY, DOD AND CIA COLLEAGUES WAS TO GET
OUT FAST AND NOW. . . . IT IS ESSENTIAL . . .
FOR YOU TO SPEED UP THE MOVEMENT OF
AMERICAN CITIZENS OUT OF VIETNAM. . . .[2]

On April 21, after a heroic defense, the ARVN abandoned its last stronghold—the city of Xuan Loc, thirty-eight miles from Saigon. It was then apparent Saigon itself was doomed. President Thieu was finally persuaded to resign. Up to the very end, he defended the record of his administration, and laid the blame for failure on America's abandonment of his country.

Saigon, on the verge of complete collapse, bustled now with people in despair. For weeks, all flights out of the city had been booked. Now desperate Vietnamese, fearing for their lives, tried anything to secure a passage out of their country.

On April 27, the first communist rockets landed in Saigon. Soon thereafter, the remaining ARVN troops abandoned their positions and their weapons, fleeing in terror to evacuation points in the city. The once-impregnable airport at Da Nang fell on April 29. The U.S. embassy had been forced by the advancing NVA to coordinate a hasty evacuation by plane and boat. In the panic that ensued, South Vietnamese soldiers had shot civilians who had attempted to climb aboard ships before them, and raped a number of women.

On April 29, at 11:08 A.M. Vietnam time, the Seventh Fleet of

An A-7 Corsair takes off from the USS *Enterprise* to provide cover and support for the evacuation of Saigon, April 1975. (U.S. Navy photo.)

the United States Navy, under orders of President Gerald R. Ford, began Operation Frequent Wind—the aerial evacuation of Saigon. By 9:00 P.M. that night, 5,000 Americans had been evacuated from Tan Son Nhut airport. Panic-stricken civilians had to be held at bay by U.S. Marines while the planes were loaded.

The marines continued the evacuation from the embassy compound itself, the former seat of U.S. power in Indochina, until 5:00 A.M. on April 30. The helicopters managed to remove another 2,100

American sailors on the USS *Blue Ridge* push a South Vietnamese helicopter overboard. During the evacuation of Vietnamese refugees, so many pilots flew helicopters to the ship that some had to be pushed into the sea to make room for others to land. (U.S. Navy photo.)

NVA tanks crash through the gates of the presidential palace in Saigon. (Francoise Demulder/Gamma.)

people, including many South Vietnamese government officials who worked closely with the Americans. Thousands of Vietnamese sought to join the helicopter evacuation. Many tried to push through the gate of the embassy or climb the high fence surrounding the compound. Marines struck out with their rifle butts in a desperate effort to maintain order. Thousands who had assisted in America's crusade in Vietnam were left behind. Their fate was up to the victors, who, as the last helicopter was leaving the roof of the embassy, were on the verge of breaking down the gates of the presidental palace.

The surrender, what there was of it, took place that morning. A Vietcong flag had gone up outside the palace. Colonel Bui Tin, a thirty-year veteran of war in Vietnam, accepted the surrender of South Vietnam from General Duong Van Minh, the same man who had been instrumental in the Diem coup of 1963. The communists' dream of a unified Vietnam under their domain was now a reality.

What, when all was said and done, had the Vietnam conflict wrought? The cost of the war, in terms of both human suffering and material resources, was appalling. The Vietnamese people, of course, had borne the brunt of the suffering. The Vietcong and the North Vietnamese armed forces alone lost an estimated 600,000 men in their fight against America and South Vietnam. No reliable estimates are available for the number of wounded the communists suffered. South Vietnam lost 223,000 men killed in action. An estimated 365,000 Vietnamese civilians, north and south, were killed.

In addition to the frightful human cost, the war disrupted the economy and social structure of the country as no event had before, crippling a proud people's march toward prosperity. Thousands of peasants had been stripped of their land and possessions, and the landscape of a beautiful nation had been horribly scarred by years of war. Today, the Vietnamese nation is among the poorest on earth. City life is dreary. Buildings in Hanoi and Ho Chi Minh City, formerly Saigon, are left to decay. New construction is at a virtual standstill.

When the North Vietnamese took over in 1975, they promised freedom and new prosperity for all Vietnamese. Sadly, they have failed to deliver on their pledge. As it turned out, 400,000 South Vietnamese, many of whom had no close relationship to either the Americans or the Thieu government, were shipped off to "reeducation" camps. Many who survived the trek to the camps died soon afterward, the victims of deplorable working conditions which compared to the concentration camps of Hitler's Germany. No reliable figures are currently available, but some sources have estimated that as many as 100,000 "undesirables" remain in camps in the late 1980s.

With their long struggle over, the North Vietnamese communists looked to expand their control over Indochina beyond the borders of Vietnam. In December 1978, after the Khmer Rouge (Cambodian communists under Pol Pot) had exterminated more than one million of that nation's eight million people, Hanoi invaded Cambodia. They stayed more than ten years. Laos, too, has become little more than a satellite state of Vietnam. Despite the abject poverty of the Vietnamese people, Hanoi's army is one of the largest and most ferocious in the world today although the government plans to withdraw all troops soon. Its primary purpose is the preservation of Vietnam's Indochinese empire. The government in Hanoi now depends heavily upon Russian aid.

Pham Van Dong, the prime minister of Vietnam in the early 1980s, got to the heart of his country's problem in an interview he gave to the historian and journalist Stanley Karnow: "Yes, we defeated the United States. But now we are plagued with problems. We do not have enough to eat. We are a poor, underdeveloped nation. *Vous savez*, waging a war is simple, but running a country is very difficult."[3]

It has been estimated that one million Vietnamese fled their native land after the communists assumed power. Most fled in rickety boats, terrified at what Vietnam would be like under communist control. While some of these refugees made it to the shore of Thailand or other neighboring countries, thousands had to be rescued from the sea. Thousands more left Vietnam never to be heard from again.

The costs and consequences of the war for Americans do not compare to those for the Vietnamese, but are considerable nonetheless. More than three million men and women served their country in Vietnam; 57,690 were killed, and more than 303,000 were wounded.

The suffering of Vietnam veterans and their families, however, goes beyond numbers. Unlike veterans of America's other wars, the American serviceman in Vietnam came home alone. There were no parades, no celebration of his sacrifice. The unfair image of the vet as a baby killer and a social misfit did not fade easily. For many years after the war was over, veterans were seen as emotionally unstable, incapable of readjusting to the real world outside the jungle.

Just as historians and other scholars have struggled to understand the important issues of our war in Vietnam, veterans have grappled with the meaning of their personal experiences in a distant and bloody conflict. The overwhelming majority of those who served

A happy group of Vietnamese refugees are picked up at night by the USS *Towers*. Many refugees were not so lucky. (U.S. Navy photo.)

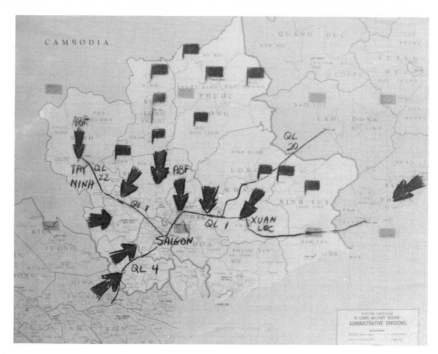

This map, which hung in Colonel Harry G. Summers's office in Saigon in April 1975, reveals the position of NVA units as they closed in on the city. (Courtesy Harry G. Summers, Jr.)

have put the horrors of their war behind them and have gone on to make their varied contributions to American society. But a significant number remain crippled and haunted by their memories. Many are embittered, believing they were tricked into fighting a war they were not allowed to win by a government that had no clear objectives. The adjustment problems of many veterans have been compounded by frustration over the lack of public recognition of their sacrifice and governmental indifference to their needs and concerns.

Myra MacPherson, in her book *Long Time Passing*, reports that between 500,000 and 700,000 veterans have suffered from symptoms of a psychological malady called post-traumatic stress disorder, or PTSD. The symptoms include depression, nervousness, reexperiencing of combat incidents, and a sense of "survivor guilt" at having made it through Vietnam alive when so many did not.

Obtaining funding from the government for treatment of PTSD and other Vietnam-related medical problems has not been easy. Perhaps the best-known stuggle of American veterans has been the one to gain compensation for health problems arising from exposure to Agent Orange, a defoliant used extensively throughout Vietnam.

There is much evidence to suggest that exposure to the defoliant causes skin rashes, birth defects in children, and cancer.

Immediately after the fall of Saigon, Americans shared a sense of relief that an agonizing chapter in their history had come to a close. In the second half of the 1970s, the war was anything but a popular topic of conversation. The entire nation seemed too exhausted and torn apart to look back and learn from the multitude of mistakes that had led to the first significant military defeat in American history.

Since the early 1980s, however, scholars, journalists, students, and policymakers have been asking all sorts of questions about a war no one seemed able to explain. Slowly but surely, the Vietnam War has become a part of our living history, a tragedy that sheds light on twentieth-century America's hopes, dreams, and values.

Vietnam has in fact become an important reference point in all discussions of America's role in the international community. When should America bring its awesome military power to bear? Under what circumstances, if any, should we use force to defend our interests in Europe, in Central America, in the Middle East? What will the costs of intervention be? Whenever these questions are asked in Washington, or in American living rooms around the nation, the Vietnam experience must be considered.

The truth is that the Vietnam War changed America and her people. Back in 1961, President Kennedy had spoken of a confident nation that would "bear any burden . . . to assure the survival and the success of liberty."[4] Believing that Americans had the right and the power to do just that, we fought a long futile war in a faraway country we knew almost nothing about. When it was over in 1975, neither the American people nor their leaders showed any inclination to enter into other military adventures on foreign soil. After Vietnam, the costs and difficulties involved in shaping events beyond our borders weighed heavily upon the national conscience. There were few indeed who believed the United States had the moral or material resources to play the leading role in global politics. We could no longer be the policeman of the free world, fighting off communists wherever they appeared.

We come now to a crucial question that has been asked many times since 1975 by generals, politicians, and ordinary citizens: Why did we fail in Vietnam? A staggering number of theories have been put forward to explain how the United States was humiliated by North Vietnam, a country with a small industrial base and scant resources. Many of these ideas were formed when passions were still high and clear thinking difficult. Some historians on the left of the political spectrum have seen our failure as the inevitable result of American greed and corruption. Our effort to help South Vietnam, in their eyes, was really designed to expand our empire and exploit the Vietnamese. The communists won out because they represented the legitimate will of the Vietnamese people. A few evil men in Washington conspired to rule Vietnam, and the American people were tricked into believing that their country was fighting for democracy.

Such a theory, however, does not account for many of the war's complexities. The validity of the leftist argument is challenged by the behavior of the communist regime since it gained power. For in establishing their own empire in Indochina, the Vietnamese have clearly placed their ambitions for power and control over the interests of their people. And the leftists fail to recognize that many early supporters of America's intervention in Vietnam had the very best of motives.

So-called revisionist writers on Vietnam have interpreted the conflict as a war of external aggression, not as a civil war among Vietnamese. They view the cause we fought for as a noble and just effort to protect people who did not want to be controlled by Hanoi's communists. The revisionists believe that the antiwar activists' vision of the war as a hideous evil, coupled with the media's focus upon American atrocities and miscalculations, created an inaccurate picture of what was at stake in Vietnam, thereby turning most Americans against continuation of the conflict. Some historians believe, along with General Westmoreland, that we could have won if the politicians had not placed so many limitations on the military effort.

Other analysts have focused upon the lack of coordination of the American effort in Vietnam. Bureaucracy got in the way of accomplishing our objectives. The services quarreled with one another constantly, and in any event were not properly trained to fight the kind of war they encountered. There is some truth to this argument, but it alone does not really explain the failure. Even if we had developed a more effective way to prosecute the war, it would not have solved the considerable political difficulties of South Vietnam described throughout this book.

A number of scholars have laid the blame for failure at the door of the various presidents, particularly President Johnson, for not realizing that each escalation—first in aid, and then in troops—only drew the nation deeper into a quagmire from which there would be no victorious return. But it is hindsight that makes Johnson's—and indeed all the American presidents'—blunders seem inexcusable. For one of the disturbing things we see in trying to recapture the reality of the world the key decision-makers lived in is how few *good* choices there were to be made in Indochina, given the role America had chosen for itself after World War II. It was a matter of escalating in Vietnam or facing humiliation, and possibly new military challenges around the world. The cost of increasing aid or the number of American troops always seemed more palatable than the cost of pulling out in disgrace. And so the war dragged on.

Colonel Harry G. Summers, Jr., a decorated veteran of both the Korean War and the Vietnam War, has argued persuasively in his *On Strategy* that the outcome might well have been different if U.S. troops had been used to block the flow of men, equipment, and supplies into South Vietnam and had left the pacification of the villages up to the only people who had a chance to succeed: our Vietnamese allies.

Colonel Summers also believes that American defeat stemmed from a fundamental misunderstanding in America of what war is all about. Under Secretary of Defense McNamara, American planners produced hundreds of thousands of pages of studies and statistics about fighting in Vietnam. Seminars were held, attended by brilliant captains of industry and university professors, to determine how to proceed. But the wisdom of the great Prussian strategist Karl von Clausewitz, who said that success in war depends upon that "remarkable trinity—the people, the army, and the government," was simply forgotten. The passions of the people are "the engines of war," and without their support, the venture is doomed to failure from the start.[5]

As we have seen, the various presidents who made America's Vietnam policy put little emphasis upon drumming up popular support for the war effort. President Johnson, in fact, deliberately tried to keep the war from heating up into a passionate issue for the American people. "The intensity of our will," Colonel Summers has written, "was kept deliberately low, and our political motives and objectives, cloaked in high-sounding generalities, were never made clear to the American people."[6]

That the American people ultimately lost the will to fight in Vietnam, then, is hardly surprising. They were never presented with a clear objective that seemed worthy of the sacrifice necessary to win. Their government had conducted a war under the illusion that victory was possible without popular support.

There was, when all was said and done, a tremendous arrogance in the men who conducted America's longest war. They could not imagine that a country with the moral, political, and economic resources of the United States could not have its own way in Vietnam. It was arrogance, too, that blinded them to the realities of life and of war in Indochina. And so America fought on, underestimating a determined enemy and overestimating its own capacity to fight a complex war and build a nation at the same time.

A view of the Vietnam War Memorial in Washington, D.C. "The Wall," which lists the name of every American killed in Vietnam, was at first highly controversial. Today it is universally recognized as a fitting—and extraordinarily moving—testament to those who paid the ultimate price for America's war in Vietnam. (U.S. Air Force photo.)

In the later years, as their quest to put an end to a national nightmare grew more desperate, they began to hide the disturbing truths about America's war from the people, from Congress, and even from themselves. In so doing, they betrayed the very ideals that Americans had been fighting and dying for in the first place.

America is still paying a heavy price for their tragic miscalculations.

Selected Chronology of the Vietnam War: 1950–1975

1950

May 8: The United States announces it has agreed to supply arms to the French in their war against Ho Chi Minh's Vietminh.

December 23: The United States signs a mutual defense assistance agreement with France, Vietnam, Laos, and Cambodia.

1951

February: The North Vietnamese establish the Lao Dong, or Workers Party, as a replacement for the Communist Party. In fact it is the same organization, headed by Ho Chi Minh.

September 7: The United States signs an agreement to provide direct military and economic aid to the government of Vietnam.

1952

November: Dwight D. Eisenhower is elected president of the United States. By this time the United States is paying for as much as one half of the French war effort.

1953

May 20: General Henri Navarre assumes control of all French forces in Indochina.

December: Vietminh challenge French troops in Laos.

1954

January 25: Representatives of Britain, France, the United States, and the Soviet Union agree to attend a conference to discuss an end to hostilities in Korea and Indochina.

March 13 to May 7: The battle of Dien Bien Phu ends with Vietminh victory.

June 1: Colonel Edward Lansdale, USAF, arrives in Saigon. Officially an assistant air attaché at the U.S. embassy, in fact he runs paramilitary operations against the communists for the CIA.

189

June 16: Bao Dai selects Ngo Dinh Diem as prime minister of South Vietnam.

July: The Geneva Agreement ends hostilities in Indochina and divides Vietnam into two nations at the 17th Parallel.

September 8: The Southeast Asia Treaty Organization (SEATO) is formed. Its members include the United States, Britain, France, Australia, New Zealand, Pakistan, Thailand, and the Philippines.

October: French forces leave Hanoi for the last time.

December: China agrees to provide aid and equipment to Hanoi.

1955

April: Diem fights and defeats rival political factions in Saigon.

July: Ho Chi Minh goes to Moscow, and negotiates successfully for Soviet help in the war for unification that is soon to follow.

October 23: Diem defeats Emperor Bao Dai in a referendum and proclaims the Republic of Vietnam with himself as president.

1956

February: The French government announces that it will withdraw its troops from Vietnam at the request of President Diem.

June: The Political Bureau in Hanoi calls for armed struggle in the south. The directive calls for buildup of both military and political forces in South Vietnam.

1957

October: Communist insurgency begins in South Vietnam under orders from Hanoi. Emphasis is placed upon terrorist activities. By December, communists have killed more than 400 government officials.

1958

June: The communists establish a command structure in the Mekong Delta region.

1959

May: The North Vietnamese establish Military Group 559, designed to infiltrate men and war equipment and supplies down the Ho Chi Minh Trail.

July 8: Insurgents attack the South Vietnamese military base at Bien Hoa, killing two American soldiers. Major Dale Buis and Chester Ovnand are officially the first two Americans to die in the Vietnam War.

December: The Laotian crisis surfaces, as communist and anticommunist forces battle for control of the country.

1960

November 8: John F. Kennedy is elected president of the United States.

November 11: Diem thwarts a coup attempt.

December 4: U.S. Ambassador Durbrow, frustrated with Diem's inability to reform his political and economic policies, informs Washington that the United States may in the near future have "the difficult task of identifying and supporting alternative leadership."

December 20: Hanoi forms the National Liberation Front to serve as the governing body of the Vietcong throughout South Vietnam.

1961

May: Vice President Johnson visits South Vietnam and advocates increasing aid to its government. The Geneva conference on Laos begins.

May 11: President Kennedy agrees to send 400 Special Forces troops to Vietnam, along with 100 other advisers. They will train South Vietnamese to conduct covert operations in North Vietnam and in Laos.

October: Two presidential advisers, Maxwell Taylor and Walt Rostow, visit South Vietnam and recommend the introduction of American combat troops to check the growing insurgency.

1962

February 4: The first U.S. helicopter is shot down in action.

February 6: The United States forms Military Assistance Command Vietnam (MACV) in Saigon; major buildup of advisers begins. By June, approximately 12,000 U.S. military men are in the country.

1963

January 2: At Ap Bac in the Mekong Delta, ARVN troops are defeated by Vietcong units. The defeat shows the glaring weaknesses of South Vietnam's army.

February 1: Official beginning of Operation OPLAN 34-A, a complex series of covert operations against North Vietnam run by U.S. military.

June 11: The Buddhist monk Quang Duc commits suicide by setting himself ablaze in protest against the oppression of the Diem regime.

November 1-2: Duong Van Minh leads a successful coup against Diem; Diem and his brother, Ngo Dinh Nhu, are killed.

November 22: John F. Kennedy is assassinated in Dallas. Lyndon Baines Johnson becomes president.

1964

January 30: General Nguyen Khanh assumes power in Saigon.

March: Secretary of Defense Robert McNamara visits Vietnam, announcing U.S. support for Khanh.

March 1: A presidential adviser, William Bundy, recommends that some sort of congressional resolution be obtained so that the administration will have more leeway in forming its war policies.

April: Hanoi, anticipating the need for additional troops in the south, sends construction battalions into Laos and Cambodia to expand the Ho Chi Minh Trail network.

August 2: North Vietnamese navy boats attack the USS *Maddox*, an American destroyer, in the Gulf of Tonkin.

August 4: A second incident of North Vietnamese boats attacking American craft is reported to Washington, but never confirmed.

August 7: The U.S. Congress passes the Tonkin Gulf Resolution.

October 30: Vietcong attack Bien Hoa air base, where Americans are stationed.

1965

February 7: Vietcong attack a number of American installations, leading to President Johnson's ordering of air raids against North Vietnam.

March 8: Two U.S. Marine battalions land at Da Nang, the first American combat troops in South Vietnam.

April 7-8: Johnson proposes a massive development plan to the North Vietnamese in exchange for peace; North Vietnam rejects the offer.

April 25: Johnson announces that General William Westmoreland will become head of MACV on June 20.

June 4: Air Marshal Nguyen Cao Ky becomes head of GVN war cabinet.

July 28: Johnson approves General William Westmoreland's request for an additional forty-four battalions of American combat troops.

October: U.S. troops defeat North Vietnamese in the Ia Drang Valley in the first major battle of the war for American troops.

December 25: Johnson suspends bombing of North Vietnam, hoping to bring the communists to the negotiation table.

December 31: By this date, there are almost 200,000 U.S. troops in Vietnam.

1966

January 8: Senator Mike Mansfield, after returning from Vietnam, offers a bleak assessment of a war that has now spread to Laos and Cambodia to the Senate Foreign Relations Committee.

January 31: The United States resumes bombing of North Vietnam.

February 16: The World Council of Churches proposes an immediate cease-fire in Vietnam.

April 1, 1966: Vietcong set off a bomb in a Saigon hotel which houses American troops, killing three Americans and four South Vietnamese.

April 11: The Johnson administration admits for the first time that South Vietnamese political problems are interfering with military operations.

May-June: Protests by Buddhists in Da Nang leave that city in a state of virtual anarchy; Ky sends in troops to quell the violence.

June 1: Students set fire to the U.S. consulate in Hue.

June 29: U.S. planes bomb oil depots in the Hanoi-Haiphong area.

August: The House Un-American Activities Committee investigates Americans who have reportedly aided the Vietcong war effort.

October-November: Johnson confers with allies in Manila; a joint statement is issued, stressing the need for a peaceful settlement in Vietnam.

1967

January 10: Johnson asks for a 6 percent surcharge on personal income taxes in order to finance the war.

April: Antiwar demonstrations occur around the entire United States.

September 29: In a speech in San Antonio, Johnson claims the United States will stop bombing North Vietnam when Hanoi agrees to enter into "productive discussions."

October 21: Antiwar demonstrators march on the Pentagon.

November 21: General Westmoreland reports that the war has reached the point where "the end begins to come into view."

1968

January 30-31: Communists attack all major cities and military installations in South Vietnam simultaneously. The Tet offensive begins.

March 31: In a televised speech, Johnson announces that he will halt the bombing of North Vietnam except for the area around the DMZ. He also announces that he will not run for president in the upcoming election.

May 3: Johnson announces that the United States will meet with the North Vietnamese in Paris for preliminary talks later in the month.

June 27: U.S. troops withdraw from Khe Sanh combat base after lengthy siege.

1969

May 14: Richard Nixon's first speech on Vietnam as president calls for the withdrawal of all non–South Vietnamese forces.

June 10: The NLF and other anti-GVN factions form the Provisional Revolutionary Government of the Republic of South Vietnam.

September 3: The president of North Vietnam, Ho Chi Minh, dies.

November 15: An antiwar demonstration at the Washington Monument draws some 250,000 people.

1970

January 28: A Gallup poll reveals that 65 percent of the people interviewed support Nixon's handling of the Vietnam War.

March 27-28: With U.S. air support, South Vietnamese troops attack communist sanctuaries in Cambodia.

April 30: Nixon announces that American troops are pursuing communist forces in the Fish Hook area of Cambodia.

May 3: The Defense Department confirms that the United States is bombing North Vietnam for the first time since 1968.

May 4: Four student demonstrators are killed at Kent State University in Ohio by National Guard troops.

June 30: The Cooper-Church Amendment is passed by the Senate. Its purpose is to prohibit U.S. military personnel from operating in Cambodia.

1971

February 8: ARVN troops are ordered into Laos to disrupt the Ho Chi Minh Trail. U.S. planes provide air support.

May 31: In secret negotiations, the United States proposes a deadline for the withdrawal of all American troops in exchange for return of American POWs and a cease-fire.

1972

March 30: NVA troops initiate a major offensive against South Vietnam.

April 16: The United States announces B-52s and other planes have hit military targets near Haiphong and other areas of North Vietnam.

April 22: Protests over the bombing of North Vietnam erupt across the United States.

October 8: The North Vietnamese present a draft agreement calling for a cease-fire and the recognition of two government administrations in South Vietnam, one headed by Thieu, the other being the communist Provisional Revolutionary Government.

November 1: Thieu objects vehemently to the agreement, claiming that NVA troops must leave South Vietnamese territory before an agreement can be reached.

December 18: With negotiations at a stalemate, the United States begins the "Christmas bombings" of the Hanoi-Haiphong area.

1973

January 17: Nixon, in a private letter to Thieu, warns that refusal to sign the agreement negotiated by Kissinger and Le Duc Tho in Paris (which allowed NVA troops to remain in South Vietnam) would mean an end to U.S. support of his government.

January 25: Representatives of North Vietnam, South Vietnam, the Provisional Revolutionary Government (the Vietcong representatives), and the United States sign the peace agreement.

March 29: The last sixty-seven American POWs fly out of Hanoi.

July 1: The Fulbright-Aiken Amendment is passed by the Congress, prohibiting the appropriation of funds to "finance directly or indirectly" combat activities by U.S. forces in North Vietnam, South Vietnam, Laos, and Cambodia.

1974

January 4: After communists initiate attacks on ARVN camps, Thieu declares, "The war has restarted."

August 6: The House of Representatives cuts aid to South Vietnam from $1 billion to $700 million.

August 9: Richard Nixon resigns the presidency of the United States; Gerald Ford becomes president.

1975

March 10: The final offensive begins, as communist troops attack Ban Me Thuot.

March 19: Quang Tri Province, the northernmost province in South Vietnam, falls to communists. ARVN troops are routed as they retreat toward Da Nang.

April 1: The ARVN yield the entire northern half of South Vietnam to the communists.

April 8-20: The battle of Xuan Loc takes place, in which one ARVN division holds off three NVA divisions until April 20.

April 12: President Nguyen Van Thieu resigns.

April 17: Cambodia falls to Khmer Rouge (Cambodian communist) forces.

April 29: The NVA attack on Saigon begins. Corporal Charles McMahon, Jr., and Lance Corporal Darwin Judge, both U.S. Marines, are the last two Americans to be killed in the Vietnam War. The U.S. Navy begins Operation Frequent Wind, the evacuation of U.S. personnel and selected South Vietnamese from Vietnam.

April 30: The Vietnam War ends with the capture of Saigon by communist forces.

Further Reading

VIETNAMESE HISTORY, GEOGRAPHY, AND CULTURE

Buttinger, Joseph. *Vietnam: A Political History*. New York: Praeger, 1968.

Cady, John. *The Roots of French Imperialism in Indochina*. Ithaca: Cornell University Press, 1954.

Doyle, Edward, and Samuel Lipsman. *Setting the Stage*. The Vietnam Experience series. Boston: Boston Publishing Co., 1981.

Fall, Bernard B. *The Two Vietnams: A Political and Military Analysis*. New York: Praeger, 1967.

McAlister, John T. *The Vietnamese and Their Revolution*. New York: Harper & Row, 1970.

Nguyen Khac Vien. *Tradition and Revolution in Vietnam*. Berkeley: Indochina Resource Center, 1974.

Sheldon, Walter J. *Tigers in the Rice: The Story of Vietnam from Ancient Past to Uncertain Future*. London: Collier-Macmillan, 1969.

Smith, Harvey H., et al. *Area Handbook for South Vietnam*. Washington, D.C.: U.S. Government Printing Office, 1967.

———. *Area Handbook for North Vietnam*. Washington, D.C.: U.S. Government Printing Office, 1967.

THE FIRST INDOCHINA WAR

Fall, Bernard B. *Hell in a Very Small Place: The Siege of Dien Bien Phu*. Philadelphia: Lippincott, 1966.

———. *Street Without Joy: Insurgency in Indochina 1946–1963*. New York: Schocken Books, 1972.

O'Balance, Edgar. *The Indochina War 1945–1954: A Study in Guerrilla Warfare*. London: Faber & Faber, 1964.

Vo Nguyen Giap. *Unforgettable Days*. Hanoi: Foreign Language Publishing House, 1978.

GENERAL HISTORIES, ANALYSES, AND OTHER REFERENCE WORKS ON AMERICA'S WAR IN VIETNAM

Bowman, John S. *The Vietnam War: An Almanac*. New York: World Almanac, 1985.

Fitzgerald, Frances. *Fire in the Lake: The Vietnamese and the Americans in Vietnam*. Boston: Little, Brown, 1972.

Gelb, Leslie K., with Richard K. Betts. *The Irony of Vietnam: The System Worked*. Washington, D.C.: Brookings Institution, 1979.

Herring, George C. *America's Longest War: The United States and Vietnam 1950–1975*. New York: Wiley, 1979.

Karnow, Stanley. *Vietnam: A History*. New York: Viking, 1983.

Maclear, Michael. *The Ten Thousand Day War: Vietnam 1945–1975*. New York: St. Martin's Press, 1981.

The Marines in Vietnam: 1954–1973. Washington, D.C.: History and Museums Division, USMC.

Marolda, Edward J., and G. Wesley Pryce III. *A Short History of the United States Navy and the Southeast Asian Conflict 1950–1975*. Washington, D.C.: Naval Historical Center, 1984.

Palmer, Bruce. *The 25-Year War: America's Military Role in Vietnam*. Lexington: University of Kentucky Press, 1984.

Pentagon Papers. Gravel edition. Boston: Beacon Press, 1971.

Porter, Gareth, ed. *Vietnam: A History in Documents*. New York: New American Library, 1981.

Summers, Harry G., Jr., *On Strategy: A Critical Analysis of the Vietnam War*. Novato, Calif.: Presidio Press, 1982.

———. *Vietnam War Almanac*. New York: Facts on File, 1985.

AMERICA IN VIETNAM: 1940–1965

Burchett, Wilfred. *Catapult to Freedom*. London: Quartet Books, 1978.

Doyle, Edward, et al. *Passing the Torch*. The Vietnam Experience series. Boston: Boston Publishing Co., 1981.

———. *Setting the Stage*. The Vietnam Experience series. Boston: Boston Publishing Co., 1981.

Futrell, Robert F. *The United States Air Force: The Advisory Years, 1961 to 1965*. Washington, D.C.: U.S. Government Printing Office, 1981.

Gibbons, William C. *The U.S. Government and the Vietnam War: Executive and Legislative Roles and Relationships*. Princeton: Princeton University Press, 1986.

Halberstam, David. *The Best and the Brightest*. New York: Random House, 1972.

Shaplen, Robert. *The Lost Revolution*. New York: Harper & Row, 1965.

———. *Time Out of Hand: Revolution and Reaction in Southeast Asia*. New York: Harper & Row, 1969.

Smith, R.B. *An International History of the Vietnam War: Revolution vs. Containment 1955–1961*. New York: St. Martin's Press, 1983.

Spector, Ronald H. *Advice and Support: The Early Years of the United States Army in Vietnam 1941–1960*. New York: The Free Press, 1985.

THE MIDDLE YEARS: 1965–1968

Blaufarb, Douglas S. *The Counterinsurgency Era: U.S. Doctrine and Performance 1950 to Present*. New York: Free Press, 1977.

Braestrup, Peter. *Big Story: How the American Press and Television Reported and Interpreted the Crisis of Tet 1968 in Vietnam and Washington*. New Haven: Yale University Press, 1983.

Dougan, Clark, et al. *Nineteen Sixty-Eight*. The Vietnam Experience series. Boston: Boston Publishing Co., 1983.

Goldman, Eric F. *The Tragedy of Lyndon Johnson*. New York: Knopf, 1969.

Graff, Henry. *The Tuesday Cabinet*. Englewood Cliffs, N.J.: Prentice-Hall, 1970.

Kerns, Doris. *Lyndon Johnson and the American Dream*. New York: Harper & Row, 1976.

Johnson, Lyndon B. *The Vantage Point: Perspectives of the Presidency*. New York: Popular Library, 1971.

Kissinger, Henry. "The Vietnam Negotiations." *Foreign Affairs*. Vol. 47, January 1969.

Lewy, Guenter. *America in Vietnam*. New York: Oxford University Press, 1978.

Oberdorfer, Don. *Tet: The Turning Point of the Vietnam War*. New York: Da Capo, 1983.

Pisor, Robert. *The End of the Line: The Siege of Khe Sanh*. New York: Norton, 1982.

Rogers, Bernard William. *Cedar Falls–Junction City: A Turning Point*. Washington, D.C.: U.S. Government Printing Office, 1974.

Shaplen, Robert. *The Road from War: Vietnam 1965–1970*. New York: Harper & Row, 1970.

Stanton, Shelby L. *The Rise and Fall of an American Army: U.S. Ground Forces in Vietnam 1965–1973*. Novato, Calif.: Presidio Press, 1985.

Tran Van Don. *Our Endless War: Inside Vietnam*. Novato, Calif.: Presidio Press, 1978.

Westmoreland, William C. *A Soldier Reports*. Garden City, N.Y.: Doubleday, 1976.

THE FINAL YEARS: 1969–1975

Butler, David. *The Fall of Saigon*. New York: Simon & Schuster, 1985.

Dawson, Alan. *55 Days: The Fall of South Vietnam*. Englewood Cliffs, N.J.: Prentice-Hall, 1977.

Goodman, Allan E. *The Lost Peace: America's Search for a Negotiated Settlement of the Vietnam War*. Stanford: Hoover Institution Press. 1978.

Isaacs, Arnold R. *Without Honor: Defeat in Vietnam and Cambodia*. New York: Vintage, 1984.

Kissinger, Henry. *White House Years*. Boston: Little, Brown, 1979.

———. *Years of Upheaval*. Boston: Little, Brown, 1982.

Nixon, Richard M. *RN: The Memoirs of Richard Nixon*. New York: Grosset & Dunlap, 1978.

Snepp, Frank. *Decent Interval: An Insider's Account of Saigon's Indecent End*. New York: Random House, 1977.

Szulc, Tad. *The Illusion of Peace: Foreign Policy in the Nixon-Kissinger Years.* New York: Viking, 1978.

THE COMMUNISTS AND THEIR WAR

Chanoff, David, and Doan Van Toai. *Portrait of the Enemy.* New York: Random House, 1986.

Pike, Douglas. *Viet Cong: The Organization and Techniques of the National Liberation Front of South Vietnam.* Cambridge, Mass.: MIT Press, 1966.

Truong Nhu Tang, with David Chanoff and Doan Van Toai. *A Viet Cong Memoir: An Inside Account of the Vietnam War and Its Aftermath.* New York: Vintage, 1986.

Van Tien Dung. *Great Spring Victory.* Washington, D.C.: Foreign Broadcast Information Service Supplements 38 and 42, 1976.

Vo Nguyen Giap. *National Liberation War in Vietnam.* Hanoi: Foreign Language Publishing House, 1971.

THE ANTIWAR MOVEMENT

Cortright, David. *Soldiers in Revolt.* Garden City, N.Y.: Doubleday, 1975.

Dougan, Clark, and Samuel Lipsman. *A Nation Divided: The War at Home. 1945–1972.* The Vietnam Experience series. Boston: Boston Publishing Co., 1984.

Powers, Thomas. *The War at Home: Vietnam and the American People 1964–1968.* Boston: G.K. Hall, 1984.

Surrey, David S. *Choice of Conscience: Vietnam Era Military and Draft Resisters in Canada.* New York: Praeger, 1982.

THE WAR AS AMERICANS EXPERIENCED IT:
MEMOIRS, REPORTAGE, ORAL HISTORIES

Denton, Jeremiah A. *When Hell Was in Session.* New York: Reader's Digest Press, 1977.

Herr, Michael. *Dispatches.* New York: Knopf, 1978.

Goldman, Peter, and Tony Fuller. *Charlie Company: What Vietnam Did to Us.* New York: Morrow, 1983.

Klein, Joe. *Payback: Five Marines and Vietnam.* New York: Ballantine, 1984.

MacPherson, Myra. *Long Time Passing: Vietnam and the Haunted Generation.* New York: Doubleday, 1984.

Santoli, Al. *Everything We Had: An Oral History of the Vietnam War by Thirty-three American Soldiers Who Fought It.* New York: Ballantine, 1982.

———. *To Bear Any Burden: The Vietnam War and Its Aftermath in the Words of Americans and Southeast Asians.* New York: Dutton, 1985.

Weiss, Stephen, et al. *A War Remembered.* The Vietnam Experience series. Boston: Boston Publishing Co., 1986.

1. A PLACE CALLED VIETNAM

1. Stanley Karnow, *Vietnam: A History* (New York: Viking, 1983), 154.

2. Quoted in Alan Palmer, *The Facts On File Dictionary of 20th Century History* (New York: Facts On File, 1979), s.v. "Truman Doctrine," 370.

3. Quoted in Harry G. Summers, Jr., *Vietnam War Almanac* (New York: Facts On File, 1985), s.v. "Kennan, George F.," 213.

4. Quoted in Gareth Porter, ed., *Vietnam: A History in Documents* (New York: New American Library, 1981), 161.

2. AN UNEASY PARTNERSHIP: THE UNITED STATES AND NGO DINH DIEM

1. Frances Fitzgerald, *Fire in the Lake: The Vietnamese and the Americans in Vietnam* (Boston: Little, Brown, 1972), 69.

2. George C. Herring, *America's Longest War: The United States and Vietnam 1950–1975* (New York: Wiley, 1979), 56.

3. Ronald Spector, *Advice and Support: The Early Years of the United States Army in Vietnam 1941–1960* (New York: The Free Press, 1985), 316.

4. Spector, *Advice and Support*, 294–95.

5. Herring, *America's Longest War*, 75.

6. Karnow, *Vietnam: A History*, 253.

4. AMERICANS AT WAR: 1966–1967

1. Shelby L. Stanton, *The Rise and Fall of an American Army: U.S. Ground Forces in Vietnam 1965–1973* (Novato, CA: Presidio Press, 1985), 90–91.

2. Al Santoli, *Everything We Had: An Oral History of the Vietnam War by Thirty-three American Soldiers Who Fought It* (New York: Ballantine, 1982), 28–29.

3. David Halberstam, *The Best and the Brightest* (New York: Random House, 1972), 757.

4. Karnow, *Vietnam: A History*, 504.

5. Karnow, *Vietnam: A History*, 514.

5. TET 1968 AND AFTERWARD: THE TURNING OF THE TIDE

1. Clark Dougan et al., *Nineteen Sixty-Eight*, The Vietnam Experience series (Boston: Boston Publishing Co., 1983), 8.

2. Michael Herr, *Dispatches* (New York: Avon, 1978), 76.
3. Herr, *Dispatches*, 139–40.
4. Karnow, *Vietnam: A History*, 546.
5. Quoted in Dougan et al., *Nineteen Sixty-Eight*, 120.

6. DISSENT AND PROTEST: THE VIETNAM WAR IN AMERICA

1. Karnow, *Vietnam: A History*, 546.
2. Quoted in Karnow, *Vietnam: A History*, 396.
3. Lester A. Sobel, ed., *South Vietnam: U.S.-Communist Confrontation in Southeast Asia*, vol. 2 (New York: Facts On File, 1969), 101.
4. Thomas Powers, *The War at Home: Vietnam and the American People 1964–1968* (Boston: G. K. Hall, 1984), 103–104.
5. Karnow, *Vietnam: A History*, 505.
6. Sobel, *South Vietnam*, 394.

7. AMERICA'S ENEMY IN VIETNAM

1. Vo Nguyen Giap, *National Liberation War in Vietnam* (Hanoi: Foreign Language Publishing House, 1971), 123.
2. Fitzgerald, *Fire in the Lake*, 245–46.
3. Giap, *National Liberation War in Vietnam*, 110.
4. David Chanoff and Doan Van Toai, *Portrait of the Enemy* (New York: Random House, 1968), 67.
5. Truong Nhu Tang et al., *A Viet Cong Memoir: An Inside Account of the Vietnam War and Its Aftermath* (New York: Vintage, 1986), 268.

8. PRESIDENT NIXON'S WAR: PEACE WITH HONOR?

1. Stanton, *The Rise and Fall of an American Army*, 294.
2. Karnow, *Vietnam: A History*, 652.

9. THE FALL AND ITS LEGACIES

1. Quoted in Porter, *Vietnam: A History in Documents*, 438.
2. David Butler, *The Fall of Saigon* (New York: Simon & Schuster, 1985), 263.
3. Karnow, *Vietnam: A History*, 27–28.
4. Karnow, *Vietnam: A History*, 14.
5. Harry G. Summers, Jr., "What Is War?" *Harper's* (May 1984), 77.
6. Harry G. Summers, Jr., review of *Big Story* by Peter Braestrup in *The New Republic*, vol. 188, no. 5 (February 7, 1983), 27.

James A. Warren was born in Providence, Rhode Island. He attended the Moses Brown School and graduated from Brown University with a Bachelor of Arts degree in history. He now lives in Brooklyn, New York, and works as editor of adult and young adult nonfiction books at Facts on File.

American history has always been of special interest to Warren. His work as editor on books about particular aspects of the Vietnam War led him to realize the need for a concise, one-volume account that would put the events of the conflict into context with the major military and political issues raised by U.S. involvement. He felt that readers, particularly young readers, would benefit from beginning with an overview before delving deeper into the twenty-five-year history of a "military action" that has had such profound effect on a great nation.